Maria,

TIME VANISHES...
LIKE A ROSE

My Dear friend from Harlem.

Love You,

Theresa Medici

Theresa Medici

Time Vanishes Like a Rose

Printed in the United States of America

First Printing, 2019

ISBN 978-0-359-47960-3

Lulu Press Inc.

www.Lulu.com

Table of Contents

Introduction

Introduction

Hi, my name is Theresa D. Medici, allow me to tell you a little about myself. The name Medici derived from the Renaissance Era. The descendants of the Medici family ruled Florence Italy from the 1500s to about the mid-1700s. They were family of poets, princes, political scholars, bankers, and pawn brokers, which was known to be one of the richest families in the world at that time. Even though, I bear the Medici name and know its starting point in history, it has been difficult to trace my family's timeline down to that point in history. I have seen certain resemblances and similarities of my family's line to the portraits of "The Medici Clan", and I do believe that we are descendants of that famous family, from stories of the old.

I was born in New York City. I grew up in what was once known as "Little Italy" on the Upper East Side. It was really our, "Little Italy", the place where my family called home. My parent migrated from Italy and came to this country seeking opportunity, a new life. Even though it was hard for them to leave and come to a foreign place, they adapted quickly and learned to come to love America and the ways of this great country. They were six children and growing up during the "depression days" it was difficult, but we all survived the hardships, war, and sadness, with hard work, respect and most importantly of all as a family. Our parents worked hard, and taught us to do the same. They believe in hard work, independence, respect and family and made sure to imprint it in our heart. Their motto was with those core values we could achieve anything in this great country. As a young girl I was always very expressive and I knew what I wanted to do and an early age. I WANTED TO WRITE! I dreamt of being a Journalist. Even though, that dream didn't come into full tuition, I never lost that passion. This is the reason why we are here now. Finally, I am putting my dreams to work and expressing my feelings through writing, even if it is much later on in my life. Over the years I have learned the term "Poetic License", and have been using that concept to indirectly structure my ideas over the years by letting go and penning my ideas creativity to paper. I am single, with no children of my own; however I have lived a good life. I have learned to love through the many challenges, disappointments, sadness, and good times, through whatever, with the belief that God is with me and will keep me safe. This is what you would see if you could look into my heart! This is what you will see in my writings!

Here are some of my life's experiences in the form of poems, prose, and stories. Maybe you will laugh, maybe cry, whatever the experience, I am grateful just to share my innermost thoughts and feelings with the world... to share my passion. But first let me acknowledge all the friends and family for the lifetime of memories, for without them this would not have been possible. There is always much more to one's life than what is seen, for those of mine that was unseen let my words bear those truths.

What America Means To Me

A – ABUNDANCE
M – MIGHT
E – ENDURANCE
R – READY
I – INDEPENDENCE
C – COMPASSIONATE
A – ALL TOGETHER

America, America, is what we stand for
We take so many things for granted
Is that who we really are?

Always fighting for our Country to unite
From the immigrant, the poor, and sublime
To go forward and fight with all our might

One can't explain our New York City
You must be a part of this great Metropolitan City
To feel its energy, life, warmth and the love
We feel to embrace each other in time of need!

Being a true New Yorker and part of the USA
All through my life, I heard people say!
OH! You're from New York? With a sneer
How awful it must be for you!
I felt anger inside and it made me mad!
I felt like I was from Barney and Clyde!

Defending my city, all the time
Did I take it personally?
Damn right I did! This is my home town!
Fury and outrage, was within me always
When traveling outside of my city
It was always the same awful remarks!
But no matter how far I traveled and how beautiful

Introduction

the outside world was, none can compare
to The City that never sleeps
New York City, USA

This City is made up of every Culture in the world
Can anyone wonder that awesome feeling we feel?
How we can sustain to get along with one another?
Freedom is our answer, we are taught to respect
each other, in spite of our differences.

The wonder of the world New York City!
We stand high and tall, not only in our
tall towers but in our spirit!

Why is it the wonder of every other city?
It truly is the, "City that Never Sleeps"!

Nowhere can one travel and find every desire
that one can imagine! Food, drink, music, and
Entertainment any hour of the day or night!
Strolling along a river, skating, or just sitting
and gazing at the wonderful skyline

There are all kinds of people walking by
They may nod or say "hello"
Or maybe not at all
We are always running somewhere
To catch a train or a bus
Hurrying to get home, so not to be late

Are we so hated across the seas?
In those faraway places, that we can't even say their names
If they understood who we really are
They would understand our culture, and
embrace this country with love!

Our Country was founded on immigrants migrating
from all over the world

Time Vanishes Like a Rose

To create, build, and not destroy
Achieving, playing, crying, sadness and laughter
Always challenging, exploring, from the depths
of an ocean to outer space into infinity!
This is who we are.
Going forward to build our
country and the future children of tomorrow

We will come together rebuild our towers
In a wave of strength with the "glory of god"
For… God Bless America

The Terrorists

T- TREACHEROUS
E- EVIL
R- RACIST
R- RADICAL
O- OPPRESSIVE
R- RATS
I- INTIMIDATE
S- STRIKE
T- TREASON

Are we so hated across the seas?
In those faraway places, we can't even
say their names!

If they understood who we really are,
They would understand our culture, and
we would embrace them with love!

Those poor, ignorant, starved people who
you will be blinded by fear and degradation
If they had one ounce of our freedom, love, compassion
We would open our doors, to all who want to be free!
They would put down their arms, and join us
in America to love one another... not hate

It's sad to think the terrorist conjured
up their own meaning of "God"
What mad men, could believe that killing
innocent men, women, and children, would achieve
their place and rise up to the gods, and take them
up to Valhalla, to be adorned by virgins!

They have come from the dark ages, holes, caves
These poor and fearful people are hiding
like rats, from humanity

Time Vanishes Like a Rose

I can only think that where they hide, lives the Devil
and the evil that exists today!

What a pity, they will never see the love of life
They do not have strength, foresight and freedom
Most of all the freedom and love that
Exists in every phase of our existence America

What have you achieved?
No mad man will tear us apart
Our tower has fallen, but we will prevail!

It's so sad you and your people
Will never know freedom or feel
What it is to be an American

The devil never wins! You will be lost in Hell
only to burn and be left in limbo
Yes, there is "anger" and sadness, but this too shall pass
And we will survive to become a greater country still!

Suicide is forbidden in the eyes of God
This can't be the same God you worship

No God has ever condoned mass murder

I know our beloved people, who lost their lives
on September 11, 2001, will never be forgotten
Their souls and spirit are in God's hands, safe, and sound
God bless America

Introduction

My Recollections of World War II

It's May 29, 2011
What a long time it must seem to have been for our heroes
from World War II, the brave men and women that are left
behind today

I would like to go back to the first time I was told that we were
at
war in our country
It was a public school in my area, located in New York City
We were attacked at Pearl Harbor on December 7, 1941

The children were assembled in the auditorium
The principal came in and instructed us to sing the National
Anthem, in addition to God Bless America
She told us that we were at war with Japan

We did not question any motives or what it was all about, not
really
Knowing what the war was all about either, was the scariest
feeling as a young child to hear this awful news
Can anyone for sure know what was going to happen?
All I could think about was, were we going to be bombed in our
homes?
All children were terrified

So, we sang and prayed for our country!
Even recited the Pledge of Allegiance
Was the words we sang threat to our society?

I came from the 1st generation of Italian immigrants
I am sure many others in our area will remember those
depression days
I have learned so much about my country and what we stand
for
Which we never questioned
It meant a lot to me and my family to have freedom, loyalty, to

work hard and respect for our flag and the USA

All during the war, we, as Americans, never questioned our country
We were attacked and we had to stick together and help each other
Today it's a different war, these are terrorists who hate us and want to destroy our freedom and what America stands for, from our forefathers, which we learned and those who died for our country!

Growing up, I remember we had to conserve food, and lights
We had a curfew and worked in defensive plants
My sister had to leave school and worked in one of the plants making bolts, screws, and parts for our planes
She took a train out to Long island from New York at 4:30am to do her part for her country
We did not cry or complain, we never questioned it
We conserved our lights and helped one another throughout the neighborhood
Times were really tough, we did not own a television set, there were no cellphones, digital satellites or any of the wonderful technology we have today but we were still grateful for all we had
We relied on our radio to hear all the news, it gave us our life
At this time there was unity
Being a Democrat, Liberal, or Republican, didn't matter and..
We did not ask why! Well, we don't have to be an Einstein to figure out the reasons why!
What mattered was our freedom to live play, pray, and our freedom of speech
In addition to all the opportunities that the USA had offered us in this great country!

We all worked for our men and women in the service, and prayed
that they would come home safe to their families
It's not any different than today, the men and women who did

not return home to their loved ones...
That was a sad day for all in America!
Was it all in vain?
I don't think so

I am here typing on my computer with no one telling me what I can or cannot say because of the freedom that we have today
We hope it will stay that way for our next generation into the distant future

What has happened to America today?
Are we forgetting our loyalty to this country?
Can we ever forget 911?
We may disagree on issues, but never in my lifetime have I heard such distaste as in the past administration the awful names that were used regarding our president!
Try that in another country!
They would hang you!
What message do we send to the terrorists!
They are still out there!
There have been many presidents that have made wrong decisions, or maybe that you did not agree with, but one can speak with dignity?
That is called "Freedom"
There are many radicals that want to divide us Americans and they are here and doing it slowly
So "WAKE UP AMERICA"!
What makes these people, who have no ability or strength to run this country or to fight a war, destroy our spirit
Our country was founded on the words "Under God"
Let us keep our country the way our forefathers intended for us to live
The American way of life, freedom, liberty, love of god, and justice
for all!
I started this article about my recollection of World War II
As for today, all I can say is that... history repeats itself
This is a horrible type of war, we do know the enemy and their

agenda
It is to destroy our American way of life

Let's remember our brave men and women today and those
who fought in the past wars
Pray for today's troops these are the real patriotic heroes
They are fighting for you and me and this great country the USA
In recollection of our troops and the times of the past

God bless America and our troops!

Sharing My Work Days

1950s Antique Switchboard Operator: My Job

Hello, Good Morning, "What number please?
Lights appear, plug in, plug out, connecting to the outside world
Throwing switches back and forward, all day long
Sitting alone 9 to 5, lights beaming, buzzing phones ringing
Burning wires, makes you want to scream!

Operator, Operator, the number for, etc, etc.
Hold on sir! Will do sir! The number is **pe-6-2000** sir!
Shall I dial it for you? Yes, please! Thank you!

"Good Morning, Ninth Federal Savings, may I help you?"
"Mr. Smith please, his line is busy, can you hold?"
"No can do, call me pronto!"

Operator, a line please, plug in, pull switch and listen in if you
like "But don't get caught"

Talking, answering questions all day, ring, ring, ring operator
please Jot down, report, then give message to the boss

Lights buzzing, operator, what happen? I'm still holding on
Anger, outrage, and sooth his fury.
Jerk!
Sorry sir, line is free now thanking you for holding on
Drop dead, keep a cool head! If you must!

All day, connections to the outside world and inside too!
Today it's digital, digital, no wires, just chips, voice mail, holding
on, cell phones, walk, talk, text, ride, and read
Car crashes! Be there in a jiff, if you're lucky to live!

"the switchboard operator has been retired"

Rage

I get so angry so quickly, losing my cool
There are times I go into a rage about:
Politics, People, New York City, Lovers and Liars
Screw the Politicians they are all Whore Masters
Screw New York Gypsies Cab drivers they are all assholes who
can't read, or write, and never know where they are going
Screw all men that are liars the worst is: Bill Clinton and Hillary
Clinton
Screw men who cheat, lie and want their cake and eat it too
Those whom don't have the balls to be honest!
Screw everything that does not make sense
All I want is to be loved like Romeo did Juliette
But maybe that's just a fairytale

How Work Defines Me

Life to me was, Work, Work, Work
Energetic, willing, able, and giving
End the day completing my tasks
Work defines me, youthful, organized, charming, helpful,
attitude, poised, Per Say!

Start the day early with a smile that wears a mask
Love my coffee and roll, no butter please!
Coffee pot brewing for those who need a fix
Too much coffee makes me tick
My work is pleasure to help the needy
Contact with humans is my best attribute
I'm a people person and love to find what makes them unique
Working alone gives me the space I need to keep control
Call it what you may, is that a bad trait?

Bosses make me hateful, never say thank you or job well done!
Their home life is dull, you're their Scapegoat
It gives them pleasure for reasoning and hate
I wait for day to end, for my tasks to get done
Rushing home at last to rest, dine, linger for a while
Sleep to dream peaceful thoughts until …
Dawn arrives to start the day with my coffee and roll, no butter
please!

Cinderella That's Me!

Call me Cinderella!
Cinderella was my Name!
Young, innocent, full of vitality, willing to sustain
Master of dirty dishes, clean windows, toilet bowls
Bed sheets in place, clothes washed and hung out to dry
On hands and knees
Scrubbing floors, making them shine
This is not to be funny, this was not for the love of money
In my teenage life, never knew what to do!
Complaining, was blaming, but to who?
Up the stairs, down the stairs, cleaning
Sweeping, dusting hallways, voices calling, and calling
"Cinderella, Cinderella, Where are you?"
Thought it was all a game, and funny too!
This not funny, laughing, I did not!
Complaining, was blaming, but to who?

My duties were my mom's and pop's, depression days
My mom was the angel..
Pop was the Dark side
Survival was to suffer
Dysfunction was the Game
War goes on and on, understanding there was none
Defense plants, hammer nails, rivet bolts
Together to fight a war, and keep the city afloat
Times were hard and I wanted to escape
Did we survive? Yes, we did our part to stay alive
Cinderella, Cinderella, thought she would die
We did not ask why
This was the life we shared
But, family is the only key to our being who we are…
Amidst a life in despair

My Definition of Work Is "Good"

Working is a necessity for living
It provides money, everyday needs, bills, food, housing,
entertainment, pleasure, and more
The rich are fortunate
Without any toils to their day
We wake early mornings and begin to start the day
From dawn until sunset
Tedious, wash up, dress, brew coffee

Run for the bus or fight for a seat on the train
Maybe an elderly lady or gent needs to rest
We crush together, garlic on everyone's breath
It's too hot or too cold, train stops
Not knowing why, so we wait on hold
Cursing for the train to make due time

Spirts are down, life becomes dull
Waiting for weekends to rejuvenate the soul
Longing for a sunny day at a beach
To sleep late and stuff yourself with all you can eat
Listening to your favorite music
It can be Jazz, Rock and Roll or the Blues
To be with your love ones, just, relax
To your hearts content
Be happy in your work, or it becomes a drudge
Work is energy, goodwill, youthful heart
Stimulation of your brain waves
Tomorrow the sun will rise
So be grateful you're alive
So work is "Good"
Even though we wait for the weekends to rejuvenate the soul

"Betty the Tiger" My Boss

Betty was her name, the Boss or "Tiger"
How I imagined her in her abode
Sitting in her chair, waited on day and night
She was obese, tall, using her authority as her might
Empowered was her manor
Walking, striding her own high
She wore black leather boots, whip in hand, ready to strike
Cared for none, selfish, sly, and cunning
Authority was her fame without shame
Ego was her game without remorse
Maids were her thing to boss around
Never did a dish she only desired to be wined and dined
Criticism was her way; she never was satisfied with life
Her mate was a wimp he jumped to every command
While demanding a knock down or a fight
No sex or love was not in right her mind
Poor Betty
Kindness, caring, understanding, and humility she never viewed
Her kin were far removed from contact
Void!
Her sons and sisters were void of love
Piety!
Betty never knew how to comfort or console
Poor lost Betty unhappy in life
No smiles, lost soul, was her strife
Hopefully in death where ever she may be
She will rest in peace, serenity, will become her repose

The Medical Assistant

Starting the day, long nights
Phones ringing off the hook
Thoughts racing through my mind
Not knowing what was left behind
Patients call, make appointments and check log book
For time, adding a new patient, or who need a visit quick
Emergency calls, screening, hearts beating, they are in pain no
one can describe
Worry, worry, if we don't place them in for a visit
The assistant is responsible, for it is possible that they may die
Death spares no time
Making the patients stressed
Keeping them in fear
Is the worst of all death?
Crowded office full of fear
So much anxiety and tension
They all need comfort...
Me too!

While attending the medical assistant school
We must learn all we can about the human body
Trying to cope with the sick
Desire to comfort the dying
The experience provided tools, but challenged the assistant
Books, tests, courses were demanding
Being a laymen, was very devastating to me
Now I was in the business to learn the language of medicine
It became "Bible"
And to absorb 11 years
Quite a feat

Assisting the doctor with stress test
Heart patients, performing cardiograms
Blood tests, seeing male and females nude
Never ending, getting use to nudity and dying too
Our chores were: smears, earaches, ingrown toe nails, obesity

Sharing My Work Days

Never ate a thing? Why the gain?
Dust of particles in eyes and ears
Ankles puffed, sprains, splinters everywhere
Draw blood, obscure veins to try and try again
Pressure, pressure!
The amazing Doc was a cardiologist
Walked a mile to see you and put you to ease and rest
Record keeping, filing, pens, pencils
Forms to fill out, collections, bills, money due all the time
Medication in proper place, sterilize, utensils
Always to be sure, or else there will be a malpractice suit
Caring, comforting the sick, feeling anxious
Understanding the need to ease the patient's pain
The medical assistant is there to help you
Get through the day and night
Then get home to rest sleep, and start again
The next day begins where the last day leaves off and so "it
never ends"

The Messenger Phone

Best friend or foe?
Personality per say
My phone rings silently, loud or mute

Waiting day and night for a message
Tingle
Lovers call to say, "Hello" or to say "Goodbye"
Or to wish you good tidings or speak bad news
Waiting, waiting, lonely nights, so let's connect Make a Call

Dialing, ringing, no one there, it's too late so we sleep to dream
the night away
The messenger rests, it knows no time
Ring, ring, wake with fear
Is it too late?
Not wanting to hear what might be my fate
I must answer if you please
My messenger phone is a contact from afar and near.
Ringing, ringing:
Hear a voice from across the sea
Listen, comfort, and its ok I'm here
We talk, talk, and pass the time of day or night
Sometimes a whisper, sometimes we weep
The messenger phone disconnects along with my aching heart

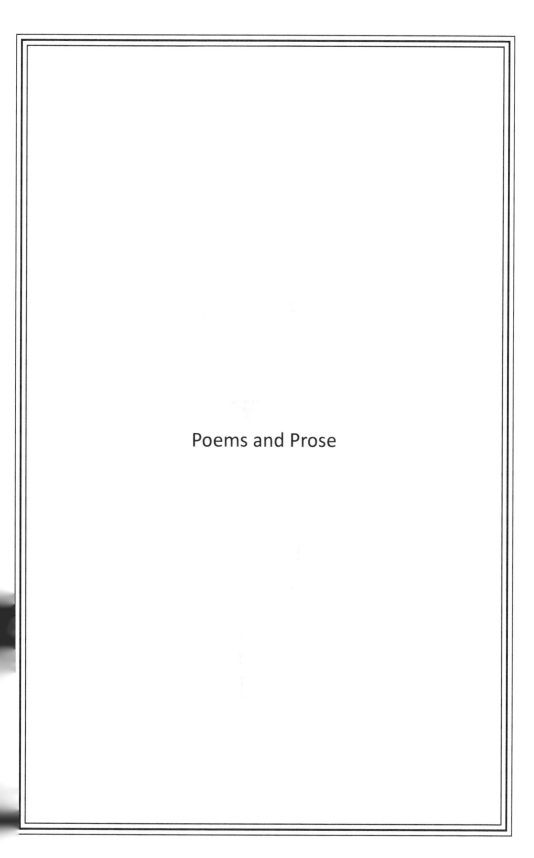

Poems and Prose

The Silence of My Mind

I lay asleep and yet awake
In sleep or slumber is my fate
In the silence of my mind
Is it real, fake or just a dream

My mind is like a tunnel
It goes on and on
To it there is no end
It is like a deep dark space into infinity
Traveling like a sailor on a lost voyage
Never knowing where I will land ...
Or will I remain lost out at sea

My body is still and yet my mind keeps ...
Roaming like a whirlwind hurricane
Tumbling, turning, running, spiraling out of control
Or am I drowning
Sometimes I try to surface to the shore
Only to be pulled down by the current
Then I'm climbing toward high ground
Only to fall from the oblivion of space
Trying to catch and lay hold on to a lonely star

Is it reality? Or is it only a dream?
Can you tell? Is it possible to wake up?
From "the silence of my mind"?

At times awake, or sleep there are ...
Monsters, dragons reaching out to me in fear!
I look around to see, only then I awake and
they disappear
Was it fact or fiction in which I am withheld in ...
The silence of my mind?

What is the mind? I see it as flowing veins
Particles of flesh, connecting

to my senses like a visual receiver
Strands of a video film only one to peer into their soul
To catch you asleep or awake
The mind is a complex, psychedelic.
Stunning and wonderful ingenuity of the brain

I seem to wake from a slumber and
I wonder where I was in time or
Was it just in the silence of my mind?

I awake and feel safe again.
"oh "what a wonderful day!"
It's reality erasing the horror
Erasing the thoughts from my mind!
Rather know it was a night of dreams
Than a reality of horrors
Does one really know: was I there
In this strange place of horror
Or in the silence of my mind

Wanting to wake to feel safe
To erase the horror thoughts
Was it in a dark place that took me …
To the unknown, into another dimension of time?
Not knowing where I was
I wake in fear of …
The silence of my mind

A Cold Christmas Night

It was a cold Christmas night
And all the animals came out to see us freeze with delight
Doug and I walked hand in hand to warm ourselves through the
winter maze
We laughed so hard to see the hummingbird sing...
The snakes crawl, and the dragon spit fire
The wood pecker pecked at the trees, bears roared
Tigers ran and the spider went up the ladder to sleep
The elephants are so gracious and grand
Oh, how we were in awe that night
To our amazement all the beautiful butterflies left their
cocoon to fly away to the moon
Then suddenly it seemed like spring
We saw the snowman so happy and tall
He led us to the iced carved deer
That would not fall
We warmed ourselves by the Marshmallow's hot fire.
We were feeling so sad, cause it was time to say ...
Goodnight to all the animals who came out
On a cold Christmas night

Stars in Flight

There are so many stars in flight!
Would you say? Millions? Billions? Trillions?
Complex is the word, for stars in space
Sometimes they look like a speck
Or seem as large as a planet, racing like a fast wind
I sit and wonder, where are they going?
I see so many falling stars, leaving their place in the deep blue
sky going nowhere
Crashing ever so gentle, only to disappear into eternity

Stars have names, did you know?
My name is in there, in space somewhere
With the Gemini in the heavens
To me every star has a purpose in our life
They could be little souls wondering about
Looking down upon us, waiting, waiting
For loved ones to appear, so they can take their flight into
space, and wander together.
Can't imagine, where they go night after night
So when you see you're star appear, say hello
Look into the dark night, so blue in the day light.
See if you can catch that falling star and take that flight, far into
the dark of night
To see where all the stars go in flight

"Far Into Eternity" My Dream!

As i lay asleep or awake, i thought it was a dream
Maybe just my mind wandering about
My life with my love was too short from start to finish
My love, soul mate, passed to soon in this life
"The Dream"
My dream begins with me waiting for my lover, Doug
To my surprise, he appears, dressed in clothes so fine, ready to take me away
He was in a car
He came to meet me
He says, "Come ", with such happiness
He was ready to take me away
We are going for a long ride far up above
He is so eager to go, looking so beautiful as usual,
and happy to get started
I said my dear Douglas. Where are we going?
Not a word, just chattering, going far up above
And he kept repeating we are going far up and away
I was wondering, what place could it be?
We both seemed happy as two peas in a pod
I was so in love, it did not matter where I was going
To my surprise we came to the top, of nowhere
It was the most breath taking view of the sky
Clouds above us, I was in awe, at all this
It had to be in heaven
Looking out from the clouds, I saw the "twin towers"
Far above the sky and the clouds, into eternity
I wanted to cry, or wake up from the confusion
I was startled, amazement, sad, staring at the towers that fell,
and turned to ashes
Up so high in space, there was a gentle little old lady, sitting at a table
She was smiling and selling coffee and cakes, and trinkets
We asked her what she was charging for the goodies
She wore a shawl over her head, smiling
She said, there was no charge for anything

You take whatever you want with you, before you go
My friend, Douglas, got me coffee and cake, and I awoke
I felt so sad, and happy too, just to be with Doug
To go to our trip to the unknown

Your Favorite Season

What is your favorite time of the year?
Spring? Summer? Winter? Fall?
Winter is cold white with snow
Windy, chilly, never getting warm
We lock ourselves in, sit by a fire gazing at the flaming red and
blue mixture of colors burn so bright
Only to watch the flames burning, fade into ashes

Here comes Spring, so quick and fast
Birds singing
Chirping so loud, they sound so sweet
They too can't wait to fly about
Spring time is for lovers... so it's said
But love knows no boundaries, to the very old
Youth's first love conquers all the passions we can't explain
When the air is filled with aroma, so sweet like scents of
mimosa

We never know what is the best time of your life or season
Reflect a while to listen, look, gaze at the trees, leaves, and
flowers
Vibrant colors that place us in awe, of the beauty in which they
possess
The leaves, trees, and flowers are waiting
They all die in a cold season that is sad
Such beauty one must see! They are awaiting Spring
To emerge, and waiting patiently to come alive again
Reflect your thoughts for the time or season
For time is of the essence

No Work

Life is work and then it's gone
To toil day after day
Now it's without pay
Three decades of work, work, work
Out of a job, what to do, where to go?
Days are long, feeling blue and sad
Think, slow down, now is the time
Search for a plan to renew oneself

Scary times, paying bills, feeding family, start again
Look for work
Retire, if you can, go with the flow
Decision, decisions, hating to decide what to do
Take time, unwind, smell the roses, read a book
Walk the beach, jump in, and swim to cool your mind
Get physical, run, walk, and talk the talk
Call a friend or loved one, don't get hooked

Missing the workforce?
Wake up at dawn
Set the clock
No work
Wow, great feeling, retire, just let go
Snow, icebound, rainy mornings, who cares
Back to bed and "the hell with work."

To Be With You!

One Night, I saw you from afar
At that moment, I felt like you belonged to me
I could not explain what I felt then
It was strange
I walked away sad
You said Hello, did I want a sip of wine perhaps
No thank you
You turned to someone else to chat

As time flew by, you appeared from time to time in many places
of fun, dancing, and laughter
You had that look of confidence about you, that...
swaggering effect, when you walked into a room
Your intelligence about life, was a plus, your challenging job, I
know you loved and did so well
Always dressed so proper, looking so neat, and fine
Colors you wore that matched to a tee

We became friends you and I, that was ok with me
As they say the game of Love and War
You chose someone else
They say time is of the essence
However, it was not my time to be with you
We danced many times together
Along, with all the others, having fun and me, loving
just to be in your presence
It was ok by me, but my thoughts were wandering
Away from a love, I lost so long ago
Did you know that you brought many memories back to me that
pierced my heart?
You were that lost love,
Again, so I thought
You were not aware of all this, but in my heart I saw all the
wonderful attributes, you possessed
Charming, heartwarming
An enigma at times

I was in awe of you
You did not know
What I was thinking!
Could this be a sense of faith that was in store for me from the
Lord above?
Part of you, does not belong to me
Your complicated life is your fate
Nevertheless, love knows no boundaries
It was not the right time for my destiny
However, life has many twists to one's path
Never thought, I would be in your arms today
Our first kiss was electrifying, arousing, and frantic
A kiss on ones lips can reveal so many emotions
The deep feeling inside, only, if both feel that butterfly effect
You know then, it's not just "The Kiss"
Do I go on? Our kiss still has that effect when we meet and it
starts all over again
Our love making is sometimes erotic, then its sweet,
comforting, as if we are one
The world outside does not exist
We are years apart, you and me
We belong together, in another time or place
I tried to say Goodbye, many times
We parted many times
It was like a sword that pierced my heart
You unleashed every emotional vibes
Passionate, joys, in my mind and body
I will always treasure the times we shared together
You will always be a part of me!
To Be With You and loving you only

A Sequel to Unrequited Lovers

Can one love and hate at the same time?
Yes you can! A women's point of view
She is emotional, sensitive, tolerant, and forgiving
Men therefore are not as emotional, more logic
They are not as forgiving, spoiled by their mothers
Non-confrontational, in important matters of the heart

The love I felt *"To Be With You"*
It was not the big picture
Even though I thought it was
Time tells many other sides to one's lover
They say love is blind, or we don't want to see beyond it
To see the real character or honor in human beings
I stated love knows no boundaries' about you and me
So I thought when I was in love
Comparing you to my lost love was also misleading to me
Your perfect clothes, ties, all your attire was about the only
thing that was real
Comparing you to him
You had only one thing on your mind
The cravings of your body
After the loving, which was fabulous, and satisfying
That is when I felt we were one together
You became another person when we parted
As you always said back to business as usual
Do all men think this way?

One can confuse lust with love
Most women do, some men don't care
Their hearts do not dedicate them
The rest you can guess
I knew he belonged to another
So why, was it not clear from the start?
He wanted the challenge to play the mind game
At any cost to win his prey
Cunning, manipulate, lying, cheating

Playing with one's mind, is dangerous
Don't you think?
When it came to honor, caring, sensitivity, and generosity
It was my lost love, who was a gentleman at all times
The game went on and on, always thinking he loves me, so he
said But he loves me not and wants me to be his friend
No way, do I believe he knows what a real friendship consists of
in our relationship
Real true friends do not hurt each other
In love or otherwise
And I never heard him say "I AM SORRY"
I was more of a friend to him, and the love, I felt
...
His indifference to my hurt feelings were so intolerable
I must let go
Try and forgive myself for being human

Holding Hands

We walk together, many times, holding hands
And stlll we are apart
You let me go
You were on your way, always wandering astray
Eyeing all you can see
Me wondering, where you are?
If, you were ok
I walk with you, time and time again
Just to look
To see what interests you, in your quiet own way
I want to feel, and understand, what's in your heart
All at once our bodies touch
And you clutch my hand in yours
Then I feel safe again!

You always guide me along the path
I tried to see what pleases you
I'm always in awe of you
Nature is a wonder, only you can see beyond
It's amazing you have that serene way about you
Then all at once you let go of my hand, for the beauty
You see takes your heart away from me
Only then, I feel lost once more
No longer secure
Yet, once again

We both see so many wonderful things along the way
Reaching for my hand again in yours
Till it's time
That we must part, still holding hands
Remembering the snow, leaves falling
The moon and stars above the heavens
Holding my hand, entwined in yours
Feeling safe once more with your hands on mine
Only to part, until we meet again

Don't Say Goodbye

We met not so long ago, it seems
It was but a fleeting moment in time
And yet I know you so well
I always felt our souls entwined

One day we are so close, touching, feeling, talking, never letting
go then in a flash of light you were gone from my sight
We dare not to talk of death we feel
It will never cross our paths
Do we know? When it's our time to part from earth
Doug, you came to me … to me one night to say Goodbye
Was that a Dream?
Or were you there?
You sat quietly by my bed and brushed my hair
For the moment, I felt safe again
In life we never said Goodbye
Always, take care, be well and goodnight.
You were always an enigma in my life
A constant frustration, pondering, doubting, was my fate
You were always, looking, wandering, and searching for some
other place in time
I wanted to say Goodbye so many times
But, my love for you was so overpowering
I needed to be with you always
You're gone from me in this life but I know you're always here
in a corner of my heart
I cannot say Goodbye

I know you wish me well and you may say, let go
And maybe love again, and move on to a new path
The sadness and pain I feel, will not let me let you go
I watched and listened to you so many times, talking about
death and what lies beyond the universe
You said when it came, you would embrace death and not be
afraid I know that is true
I was there beside you, holding your hand

Time Vanishes Like a Rose

Hoping and praying that you are happy and found your Shangri-La
I hope you can hear my thoughts
I miss your voice saying, Hello or Goodnight
Or how are you doing today
I miss your touch
Your gentle kisses, upon my lips
The quiet way you sat sipping your wine
How you would listen to me talking all the time
And you never seemed to mind
I sense the smell of you, upon me
The aroma of perfume you gave me
The outstanding ties your wore, leaving for a day's work as I always was in awe of you
I miss your quiet ways, not knowing if you were happy or sad at times
I just miss all of you

We listened to the voice of Madam Butterfly her sadness of love
Singing a note so high to reach the sky
Your love for the opera always made me cry
The passion we shared together with all the beautiful music that was created so long ago...
It will always linger on forever in time
Doug My Love,
You left me so sudden without a word only silence
I feel a lonely sadness as a part of me is missing you
Then there is anger too
Why?
God sent you to me and then took you away?
My heart tells me you are still near
Was that you in my dreams...
Or just an angel reaching out to me?
Please don't say goodbye
Just say: "So long for a While"

Can Love and Hate Be One?

Women are emotional, sensitive, and forgivable creatures
Men are logical, spoiled brats by their mamas
They are cold, never giving when it comes to a matter of the heart
The leave you at the very first start of emotion
Can love and hate be one?

Love is blind
We can't see beyond it
Love is an interlude, and then we are in a bind to its song
But before you find its true rhythm it is all gone

We women think about love
We long for love
There is only one thing on a man's mind
Can love and hate be one?

Love to men is a phantom
It appears to them and then leave
Leaves back to the outside world
Just like the falling leaves
They return after the Fall
And then are gone after Spring
We feel there is no trust
We don't know if its love or lust
Can love and hate be one?

Men play the game to win their prey
Women are alone crying
Not knowing a reply or what to say
Hearts are broken every day
Can love and hate be one?

Women confuse lust for love
Only to be left to believe
The lord above has the last say

Time Vanishes Like a Rose

Can love and hate be one?

My Expectations of Love (How We Met)

We met one winter night
It was a bitter cold Christmas season
No expectations in mind
For a lover or Mr. Right
He appeared out of the blue
Dancing, chatting, merry times
Friends, toasting, holiday cheer
All was calm and merry
Amazement, you appeared, my lover to be

First glance, you touched my heart
But, of course what was to come from the night
Never gave it a thought
That is not true
Women always know
Basic instincts we follow

Do you remember how we met?
Most romantic men do
A stranger threw a pretzel
It was meant for you
It was your attention she wanted
The silly pretzel hit me instead
Talk began between you and me
Was that fate?
One must say
Yes I do believe it so

Spoke of this and that the usual talk
Your rush Limbaugh tie was the key
Wow, did that make your day
Surprise, surprise, I knew who Rush was
The man you so adored in your politics
The usual chat, when strangers meet
Talk, work, play, travel, or cheat
Moments of time

Time Vanishes Like a Rose

Was like, we existed in another space of the universe
Our thoughts mingled like stars at night
You said so much, yet so little
For I talked too much, I think you liked that
I'll confess
I wanted you to like me
Was it the wine that made you chatter?
Or my candor for honesty, my warmth, flirtatious manner and
sincerity

We danced to our very 1st song
"The wind beneath my wings"
Then it was "The phantom of the opera"
Which was a delight
Holding me so close
Your touch…
Made my body tremble so
Never wanted to let you go
Did you feel the same?
Or was it just lust, or insane?
As women often think
No, it can't be he really feels the same

Evening ended never to know
Would we meet again?
We did not exchange numbers
Negative thoughts racing in my mind
Was it fate to meet or to let go
He was my dream man
What I wanted in a lover
Tall, eyes of brown, fair skin
He wore glasses
Cute I thought
He was exciting, bright, intelligent, and fashion was his game
He had a small sense of humor, keen
Well put together, secure, sure of life
His work was his challenge, opera was his love
A mystery man of the universe

Would he return next week
The same place?
I said I would only not to play the game
He said he would be there
The single world has many lies
Game playing and mind boggling
Woman don't know, but they venture
To taste, touch, feel, and longing to belong to the other half of
one self

Quote Noah's Arc must be in twos
Going to the new world
Is that a myth?
I wanted to run into the night
Let it all go
Was this not my fate

Time passed on I returned to meet my date
Immediately, the negative side of me pervaded
Thinking he would not be there
We did meet
He was there like a dream
Such desire waiting
I wanted you to hold me again to share that feeling
Of never letting go
Then give me a peaceful soul
Part of me feels that I will never be loved
Like Romeo and Juliette

You sent me Douglas, was that fate again?
Was I too eager to want to be loved
And afraid to search deep inside of me to know
Was it love, lust or passion?
Did we go too fast, leap into desires to fill our needs and
sorrows?
Passionate love, no boundaries, holding our bodies entwined
together
Not knowing what desires would unfold

Time Vanishes Like a Rose

Or was it just a game?
Again, did i give too much?
What's too much, or too little?
Were we soul mates?
Or should I let go
Time changes us, and death parted us
But I will always love you Douglas

Wine Tasting

Dress up, make up, hair in place
High heels, short skirts or long
Must look just as good as the wine

Stand for hours on end, set a table
Cheese, crackers, glasses, napkins for ladies
Small enough for a sip

Men and women browsing
Eyeing the wine
Tasting and smelling the aromas that suits the palate
Merlot dry, sweet Rosa, Chardonnay, tart
Smooth as bouquet's season
Wine aged in oak vats just aged in time
What are your desires or occasions for sipping wine?

Chat a bit?
What makes people tic?
Eat crackers, cheese, take a sip
Selling wine is art
Like it or not
Fun, party, dinner, or just drink
Come in browse around, chat, taste a bit of wine
Buy a bottle or two, and then my job is done

My True Adventures

The Unforgettable Trip: "Cartagena 1973"

In 1973, in the Bronx area of New York City, Maureen Kelly and I worked for a private doctor. We both were his secretaries. I was his medical assistant and Maureen did his administrative work.

Dr. Marra was a cardiologist and internist. He was an excellent physician. He was from the old school of caring for his patients, his patients came first and its very rare that you will find that dedication in today's field of medicine. Dr. Marra and his wife were like a mother and father to us. They taught us all about their family business and how to care for their patients. Maureen and I were like family while we worked the office. They both treated us like their own daughters. They even took us on paid vacations every year.

It was great! And we learned so much from traveling with them to many different countries. We would have never experience the places we got to see in our life time without them! Mrs. Marra was quite a lady. She was a gourmet cook, spoke two languages, sang opera, played piano and did just about anything you could think of in household. She also was the one who planned their vacations for going all over the world. Mrs. Marra formerly was a teacher located in the Bronx area. Mrs. Marra always took wonderful care of her husband and family respectfully. The doctor's office was located in their home, in the Bronx area. Many times we would have lunch, while we were on a break with them. I must say we had it made!

The doctor and his wife, were very generous people. We really were well fed and lunch was always a delight. One day, Mrs. Marra came into the office and said to both of us, "do you want to go to this new island in South America called Cartagena?" Even though we had never heard of this island, Maureen and I were extremely excited. We replied, "Yes. When? What do we need?". "Passports", she replied. "We will be departing in April of 1973. Dr. Marra invited his niece to join us on this trip". Dr. Marra often travelled with other doctors and friends, so this was new to us. After a long winter we were very excited and

looking forward to the sun and relaxation of a beautiful island!
The time was finally here. We left for Kennedy airport. The
flight was about 5 hours to Cartagena. We arrived in a tiny
South American airport, which the pilot would have missed if he
had blinked his eyes. We then had to take a two to three hour
bus ride to the island. As you could imagine we all were
extremely tired but that did not stop us from thinking about all
the fun we were about to have. Reluctantly, we boarded this
dirty broken down piece of junk! It was very dirty. Little did we
know we were in for some surprises. There was a policeman on
the bus and he asked us for our passports. He was not very
pleasant and had a pistol on his hip. His uniform was awful, not
like a New York police officer. He made us all nervous, we did
not know what this was all about. He said it was just a
procedure and he would return the passports to us at the hotel
later that week. Mr. & Mrs. Marra were very angry, but said,
"be calm, let's not make matters worse". So we all proceeded
to the hotel booked for us by the agency that Mrs. Marra had
faith and used for all of her travels. Upon arrival the desk
manager told us that there was no rooms for us available, "The
hotel is overbooked, I am sorry but we cannot accommodate
your party", the man behind the counter said. Now we were left
standing there hungry, tired, passport-less, sensing that our
plans were not going as well as they should have! We then
traveled to another hotel in the same area with a girl named
Melanie, whom the hotel also didn't have any room for, and
tried to make the best of an already trying situation.
This hotel horrible! The room we shared was awful. The
furniture was old and worn out. There wasn't even a lock on the
doors. What were we thinking? We were so scared at this point.
We could not sleep that night. Mrs. Marra came in to see if we
were ok, she told us not to worry,   "We will not stay here but
one night. We will register in another hotel tomorrow", she
said. If you think I am kidding, this was a brothel hotel, women
were going in and out all night long. Figure that out! The doors
were banging open and shut all night. To calm down our
nerves, we thought that it would be good to have a little drink, I
had a bottle of vodka, so all we needed was some ice and tonic.

Therefore, I called the front desk and asked if they could send us up some ice. Wrong idea! A seedy looking fella came to the room, and looked as if he wanted to get "friendly" with us. He was unhappy at my demand for him to leave, and so we shut the door behind him adamantly. We continued to have a few drinks, all the while trying to forget, that there was no locks on the door and anyone could come in at any point, at any time and do whatever to us. Needless to say we didn't sleep much that night. At least the drinks calmed us down somewhat. Well, for me it did anyway.

DAY TWO:

We all got dressed and could not wait to get out of that place. Dr. & Mrs. Marra came to fetch us they said that we were going to another hotel which was decent and clean. It seemed that all the hotels were booked, we never got into the original first class hotel that Mrs. Marra had booked. We ended up staying at a hotel, whose name I can't remember; it was located in the same area. It had an outside garden. The rooms were ok. At this point, there was not much we could do. We couldn't leave the island apparently, there was only one flight a week in and out of the island, and we had no passports. "LORD HAVE MERCY US." We wanted to leave sooner than we anticipated! No luck! We were stuck! So we decided once again, to just cut our losses and try and see as many things on this island as would could, have fun and relax in the sun. HA, HA! I thought to myself.

Mrs. Marra booked some of the tours for us to see the island. Most of the tours took us to the town of Cartagena. In Cartagena, there we shopped for jewelry and trinkets. This island was best known for their emeralds, so we all bought some little raw emerald stones. Mrs. Marra then planned a boat trip thru the marshlands. It was a small boat and a man who was a black islander was rowing through the waters. I was so scared. He said to all of us in the boat that there were sharks and alligators in the water, amongst other animals. That got me screaming all over the place. This was not my idea of fun I wanted to get off this boat cause I am frightened to death of deep water, especial being on a small boat. Anyway, we made it through the day and then went to dinner that night at a local place in town.

It was sad to see so many children live in this manner. This was a Third World Country! Very poor. The kids were running around ragged and begging for money. It was a very rural area. There wasn't any entertainment at the hotel. We visited the mines where the emeralds came from and walked around this poor town. We stayed together for a fear of what possibly could happen next. On check in at the hotel we were told that the lights would go out on occasion, so we had to carry little search lights with us. Guess what?! On the way back to the hotel that night, they did! We had to walk in the dark with our little flashlights. We were also told that the water could go off at any time. And, guess what?! You guessed it. While I was taking a shower full of soap, the water just shut off. Now just picture that. I don't know how we all didn't go crazy! Oh, what a night.

DAY THREE:

We girls decided to go to the beach. We found our way there and had to purchase straw mats for us to lie down on the sand. The beach was ok, it was very rocky. The water was not the greatest, not at all like the Bahamas, so we didn't go in the water. We just laid on our straw mats. After a while Barbara said she was not feeling well. She said her body was itchy all over? So we returned to the hotel out of fear! Once at the hotel we called Mrs. Marra to come and take a look at Barbara, she was so embarrassed to find out that some kind of sand bugs had invaded her private parts! That made all of us hysterical, and soon we were checking our own bodies. Not to long after this incident Maureen then started to feel sick, and developed a high fever. She had a virus or something, I guess, because she was throwing up and had to stay in bed for a day or two before she started to feel better. It didn't stop there, things got worse by the minute, I too got very sick. I started vomiting and was diagnosed with having dysentery. Afraid of getting too dehydrated, Dr. Marra gave me an injection to quiet down my ailment, and after about two days of rest I started to feel a little better. I must say thank god for Dr. Marra for being with us, he took care of us. I believe that if we did not have him around on this island, thing might of gotten out of hand, for finding a good doctor on this island would not have been easy. I not sure if I would have even trusted them! Who knows! If we needed to go to a hospital we would probably have been doomed. There are benefits to traveling with your own doctor, "our boss". Even Mrs. Marra wasn't feeling well, but she never complained for she did not want to alarm us. Being the great lady we knew her to be she just tried to comfort all of us.

After four days, they finally returned our passports to us. I had no idea what that was all about, even though the though had crossed my mind that they wanted to kill us and keep our passports? At this point, I didn't trust anyone, these people all seemed very weird. We all just wanted to go home to our own beds and our environment, "THE GOOD OLD USA." As expect, we all were cautious about eating, for fear of being sick again. We tried to have some fun, and be positive for the rest of the week. We went shopping in town and kept busy so time would pass by quickly. I guess the more you want time to pass by, it seems it never does! One evening, Maureen returned to her room and couldn't find her passport. So we called the police, and reported it, thinking that someone might have stolen it from her bag. We really were getting paranoid! We went out into the street, thinking that the culprit would try to sell it. Thought that it might have been this poor kid that had stolen her passport, but he picked up his shirt to show us that he didn't have it. What a nightmare, we were frightened, and even start to think that we would never leave this country. Trying to control ourselves and not panic, we headed back to the hotel. Mrs. Marra was extremely upset but tried to keep us calm, "Ok let's back track our steps". After a few moments had passed, guess what... Maureen found her passport. She forgot that she had hid it somewhere in her bag. This was not a vacation, it was a horror movie!

Time Vanishes Like a Rose

DAY SIX:

This day couldn't come fast enough. The week was up, it was time to leave! We were told that the bus would be arriving in about 2-3 hours to take us to the airport. So we packed our bags anxiously in expectation of its arrival. When the bus arrived, we were relieved. It took us about 3 hours to get to the airport. Funny, but it didn't feel as if the trip to the hotel took that long when we first arrived in Cartagena. Nervously, it was in my mind that they didn't want us to leave the island. Those 3 hours felt more like 100 hours. We traveled through the side roads, through the rural areas, stopped to eat at a shack. The food was ok, but I was focused on getting home and at this rate we never would. When we arrived at the airport there was little to no talk. We boarded our plan, and arrived safe late that night at JFK airport. Ahhhhhhhh, safe and sound. All we wanted to do was rest. Rest from the week, rest from being sick, rest from the experience, rest from the nightmare. But, Dr. Marra got sick and was hospitalized for a week with some sort of virus. The island wouldn't let us go without a fight. We never knew what exactly was wrong with him, poor guy.

Mrs. Marra reported the whole incident to the agency and the proper authorities. They were like superheroes to us and even though it was a horror of a trip we thanked Mr. and Mrs. Marra for all their patience and fortitude. I really don't know what we would have done without them being there to guide us mentally and physically through that horrible week.

What do you think of Cartagena? If asked that, I don't know what I would say. Maybe, that the island wasn't ready for travelers, or that they didn't have the facility to accommodate a fellow traveler! How about, I will never travel to South America again! In about 2011, a few of my friends went to see relatives out there, and professed that they had a wonderful time. Well good for them! One thing I know is that Cartagena was not for me. It is forever scratched off of my vacation list.

The Sailing Trip of 1990

One day in the heat of the summer in the month of august. It was a very hot summer that year, so I wanted to go sailing. Of course, I didn't own a sail boat, however, I have sailed many times with my friends that did owned some beautiful sailboats. I also had taken a sailing and power boat course in City Island and so I did have some experience out on the water. I was so desperate to go sailing. I just wanted to sail along the shores of Long Island and gaze at its beauty. So I decided to go on an adventure! I search through the papers and to my delight I found an ad in this magazine which read, "Sailing for Singles" on that Labor Day weekend. "Great, I thought! This is just right for me. I can enjoy the breeze and try and meet some new people." The article look legit and it had the gentleman's name and phone number, so I called him to find out all the particulars about this trip. His name was Tony Rocco and he was Italian, of course, with a name like that. He told me that it would cost $200.00 dollars for the trip. "Bring your own sheets, and a pillow. Food is included", he told me over the phone. Tony mentioned that he was renting a 28 foot sailing boat and that he said he was a licensed captain. I never did get a chance to see his license! We spoke a few times before the trip. He told me that there would be a lot of single people sailing with us. I wanted to be sure that this was not the Boston strangler or some other scam, but he seemed sincere. I told Tony that I had sailed many times, and that I do have experience operating power boats and sailboats because I had taken a 12 week course. I was not a novice to the whole adventure, I just really loved the water and sailing.

Before I knew it the time had come. I packed my bags and I was off! With my pillow, sheets, and a few other personals! My friends all thought I was absolutely crazy, but I didn't pay any attention to them! Mr. Rocco told me that it is was about an one hour from New York City to the docking location. I was to procced on i95 north, go through Connecticut and get off at exit 60. There I would see the harbor, with tons of sailboats stationed. So I followed his directions and after driving for about two hours I arrived at the harbor now extremely suspicious about the whole trip.   "If his directions are this off……", I thought to myself, but tired and all from the drive I kept my cool and began looking for the boat. The name of the boat was "The Dawn". I noticed a boat with that name at a distance and proceed to head toward it. A man was on the deck of the sailboat waiting for people to arrive, so I went aboard and introduced myself. He seemed nice enough, so I asked, "where are all the other people that are sailing with the group?", to which he replied, "They should be here soon". Not too shortly after that, two women and one man came on board. I did not know what was going on, I did not see anyone else but three people. Here I was 90 miles away from home and I felt a panic attack coming on. In an effort to calm my nerves I started to talk with the women, it seems the two women were friends, and the man was married to one of them. All abroad! And that was it for the weekend. No one else was coming on this trip, but us 5, including the idiot captain Rocco. He was more like Captain Bly. I wasn't the only one upset though, the others expected more people to be here as well, but in the end we decided to make the best of this trip. Our second surprise came shortly after. You know that food that was included in the price of the trip, well Captain Bly informed us that we had to pay for the food ourselves?! What? Tom, Helen, Eva and I, we all looked at each other puzzled and upset. What should we do? Kill him and throw him overboard or take off and leave the trip behind altogether? We had paid in advance, so right now we were at his mercy. Once again the decision came to make the best of the situation. This trip was going to last for four days, and our destination was Block Island. We would not be stopping anywhere else on the way there. We all got along fine, "so let's go sailing", we thought. It seemed that Tom knew about sailing and was familiar with boats as well. Thank god for that! I felt very safe with Tom at the helm!

So our adventure got started. We bought food. Eva and Helen were going to cook, I was going to help of course. We were determined to have fun. Tom and Eva were married and had some problems, so they decide to take a sailing trip. Helen was her friend, a very nice lady and we all got along fine. Poor me thinking there would be other people aboard that were single! Ha ha ha that was it! If the captain was good looking or had a nice personality, maybe I would not have minded, but he only became more obnoxious as we sailed out into the ocean, on a very hot weekend, with little to no breeze!

We started out from Connecticut around noon, sails went up, we got settled into our cabins. Mine was in the aft part of the boat, which is toward the back. It was tiny, but it was ok, I laid down on my pillow, with my sheets on the cot. Captain Bly, as we decided to call him, took the helm and powered out into the Connecticut River to our destination… Block Island. We had 4 days out into the ocean, God Help Us! When I go over this in my head, maybe my friends were right? Maybe I was crazy. Even though, I love sailing, I am kind of extremely scared of deep water. I know, I know, I know. It doesn't make sense, but I can't swim and Bly is sailing. You figure this one out, because I can't. The weather was just not cooperating with us, there was no wind at all, and it was very hot and humid, and a hazy day. Now anyone one knows about sailing knows you need wind to sail. For many hours, we had to use the motor to move on toward our destination! Thank god, he had a motor on this sail boat! Oh did I mention that it was a rented sail boat? Captain Bly rents boats and then tries to gets people to sail with him. To do this, you must have a sailing license. Well none of us ever saw his license, so who knows? He was very vague about himself, and very quiet man.

As the day went on we had drinks, and got to know each other a little better. The girls cooked a delicious gourmet meal. They lived in New York City. Eva taught dancing, and Helen worked in advertising. Tom had a business of his own. When one sails with strangers, so to speak, you get very close to each other. When you're out on the ocean it makes you feel like you never know what may take place in the next hour. Captain Bly did not want any of our food, he eat a cold and hard sandwich that he brought aboard. Weird! While we were talking, out of the blue the captain started to share some information to us about himself. He said that he was Jewish. He was adopted by Italian parents and they brought him up as a Christian. His name is Tony Rocco, but who knows who he really was! All I knew for sure was that he was a very weird person. The wind on the water was still non-existent, so we were on power all the way into the ocean. It was getting very late, therefore we stopped at another marina had dinner and continued with our notion of making the best of this trip. Other than the small talk, Captain Bly didn't really seem interested in joining us in our activities, not that we wanted him to anyway. We were still a little angry about his deception. We rested for the night and then on the following day we started out again for Block Island, still with no wind! It was another hot and humid day, seeming like no chance for a breeze to take place. Unfortunately, the shower inside our cabins didn't work, so we all had to shower in our bathing suits on deck. The captain just stood and watched us eerily, the captain was always looking at us very strangely. Tom took the helm at times and I did too. I really enjoyed sailing. We all got along very well together, except for Captain Bly.

We were now approaching Block Island. If you are familiar with the island you know that it has biking, hiking, bars, and is a great place to party. The four of us decided not to bother with the captain and that we were going to party that night. Therefore, we did! We had no idea where the captain was and where he had disappeared to on Block Island. We also didn't care too much. We all had a very nice evening on Block Island, dancing, drinking, and touring around the island. It's a really beautiful place to "get away from it all". It's quite a place to visit. We slept on board that night, and as soon as it was daybreak, we were off again. Still no wind, hot, and humid!

Tom said that he had friends in the Hamptons and maybe we could all stop there and have some fun. We all agreed to this and told the captain our plans. This was on our way back to Connecticut. When we arrived in the Hamptons, we docked the sailboat, and ditched the captain as fast as we could, we wanted to get away from Mr. Rocco, I know all this sounds mean, but this man was not honest with us from the beginning. We met up with tom's friends and had dinner and drinks and we had a very good time. We laughed all night, talking about Captain Bly. Once again we did not know where he was at that evening. When we got back to the boat later that evening Captain Bly told Tom that he wanted us to pay for the fuel. We were outraged at this and told him no way! Tom got so mad that he was ready to get into a physical confrontation with the captain, but we calmed him down and made it through the night. We talked in our cabins ignoring Bly's ignorance, about the good time that we just had, and what we would do when we reach the harbor, and then we fell asleep.

We started out the next day as the rest, with no wind, hot and humid. Not the ideal conditions for sailing, extending our time on the waters. The captain was at the helm swamped with maps. We were on deck, trying to get some sun. We were moving slowly and then I took the helm for a while. He directed me with the compass. And I followed his instructions. I stayed on that course for a few hours. We were all anxious to get home. Tom was good at sailing, and he said it was taking too long for us to get to the Connecticut harbor! So I gave him the helm to help direct us home. I was on deck, trying to sun myself, when I heard the sound of a bell ringing! It was a buoy and we were getting closer to it. I was startled. I remembered from my sailing classes, that if you hear that sound, it means danger! I tried to tell the captain that we were in danger, but he said no, we were ok. The rest of us knew that wasn't true, we started to believe that did not know how to handle this sail boat.
"LORD HAVE MERCY", I shouted. Tom and the captain were looking over the maps and the compass and realized that we were heading into the Connecticut River swamps, and we were sailing into very low waters. Tom took the helm and steered us out further away from the muddy waters. We could have hit the rocks, or got caught on them. What a disaster that would have been! We would not be able to get out of the swamps. Of

course if that had happen, we would have had to call for an emergency mayday!

Thank god! We arrived safe into the harbor. But before docking all of us made a plan to pack our belongings pillows, sheets, and clothes and get off as soon as he pulled into the harbor, we exchanged phone numbers and also left him with all the food that we had bought on board. We were going to flee like the Egyptians flight out of Egypt with all our bags in hand. We were laughing so hard, we did not know what he was capable of doing to us! When we docked, we all started out to the run way, Captain Bly was screaming at all of us saying, "WAIT, WAIT! YOU HAVE TO WASH DOWN THE SAILBOAT BEFORE YOU LEAVE! " . Tom turned red and then green like the hulk. I really thought he was going to kick his ass. He turned around to him standing on the deck, and said out loud, "fuck you! You do it yourself!". Then we all left, and never saw him again. My new motto … "NEVER GO SAILING WITH STRANGE CAPTAINS ANYMORE".   I could not stop laughing all the way home. I did keep in touch with Tom, Helen and Eva. I also continued sailing, but only with people I knew very well!

As Youth Comes to a Close 1940-1962

I grew up at 429 East 114th street, between pleasant avenue and 1st avenue. This part of town was referred to as "Little Italy", in East Harlem. I was really in love with that neighborhood and tended to do a lot of research about its background when I was younger. From what I can remember, around the early 1700s to1800s, this area was mostly made up of German and Dutch immigrants that migrated from various European countries. The name Harlem was actually derived from the Dutch country. This beautiful area, which was about 10 blocks east of 116th to 125th street, made up this Pleasant Avenue. I ways wondered why was it was called that? The area was graced with brownstones. The area had it all, a race track, trolley cars, horse racing; it truly was a great city street. I assume the German and Dutch, who lived there, thought it was quite a beautiful area as well. One block east was the East River, which ran all the way down to Battery Park. It was a beautiful river! Boats and barges ran along it constantly, working their way down the lower east side transporting all sorts of goods to the many businesses in New York City. Thinking back, I can remember that some kids even swam in that awful water, I mean it was beautiful from a distance but not meant for swimming, the water was dirty and full of tar. The boys would come home coated with black tar, you can only image how upset their mothers were at them. My older brother Frank did it once! What a mess! Many years later, in 1940, the city built the Jefferson Park and pool. It was beautiful, and everyone in Harlem was really happy to be able to swim without being full of soot afterwards. The tar days were over! Today, Jefferson pool still exist and Harlem also still has a beautiful playground as well.

We all were so very young and foolish in our youth. Reminiscing back on the good times we had of love, laughter, even sadness. Life seemed to have started in our teens. Looking back on it now, everything that I've experience growing up feels as if it were a dream, some sort of fantasy. We all have our own expectations of life but sometimes things turn out far beyond our wildest dreams.

Eventually, some people left the old neighborhood and were successful, others stayed. Oh, how they loved their "Little Italy"! I was one that left, but can't help to think back on all my dreams and desires when living there, or about my dearest friends that I left behind! I had dancing partners, lovers, all with thoughts of a tomorrow. We did not think that our paths would end up like this, however we laughed, danced, and loved in the moment. Much heartbreak occurred along the way, but at least the times that we had together were real, at times tearful, but loving and passionate. We never thought about if it would die one day or live forever. The time that I spent in our little area, which is considered East Harlem, some of my most precious memories were right there on that street called Pleasant Avenue. To all of us whom lived there as youngsters, there could never have been a more pleasant avenue. Remember, how we would walk and talk alongside of the east river that ran along side of East Harlem and continues on to Battery Park? Sure now it is considered the FDR, named after one of our presidents Franklin Delano Roosevelt but to us, we knew it as, "The East River". At the time, no one cared what it was named. We were just in awe that whether driving, walking, we could be with our loved ones and look clear from one side across to the other side of the river, seeing what seemed like foreign land, Randall's Island. How about the pier located at east 111th street? How amazing! It extended out onto the water. It was a place that we went to getaway, and dream. We used it to hold hands, and hug, having no idea that the pier was probably created for fishermen to fish. We just loved that pier. Our playground was named after Thomas Jefferson. This is where we played on the monkey bars, swings, bocce courts, and where we would roller skate. The park had a swimming pool two blocks long, this was our summer savior, not to mention the football and soccer fields. What a grand park. It was like an amusement park to us. Remember the planting grounds? How about the battles on the paddle courts? .... Most of all The

Grand "White House"! Why did the city name it the "White House"? Yes! Right smack in the midst of Thomas Jefferson playground, we had our very own "White House". It was our secret place! We spent so much time there. They held many events there, music, concerts, puppet shows, etc. It was the neighborhood's place for entertainment. The park and playground was beautiful. It was about four blocks long in total, from east 114th street to east 111th street and First Avenue. My pop and I used to watch soccer and football games there from our front room window. These events were a treat and normally held every Sunday afternoon. It is one of those special memories that I will never forget. Then there was the famous Mt. Carmel church located on east 115th street between pleasant and First Avenue, which still stands today, it's over 125 years old! I recall that every July 16th there was a great feast to honor their patron saint. On that day there was a celebration with rides, games, food, peppers and sausage, all kinds of Italian pastries and espresso. The procession of the famous Mt. Carmel Saint was carried out into the streets. Many people walked barefooted in honor of the Madonna, including my mother. Honoring the Madonna of east 115th street in NYC was one of the greatest feasts in catholic history. It went on for two weeks. There was a lot of noise, cooking and great smells of food. I sometimes wanted it to end quickly because on hot nights I just wanted to go somewhere to cool off. The church was named Mt. Carmel after a beautiful mountain that faced west, just north of the holy land midway between the country of the Jews and the cities of Gentiles. One tradition of the Mt. Carmel church was the Carmelite order. It commemorated the feast of Mt. Carmel in 1251, where it is said that the Blessed Virgin Mary appeared to a Carmelite priest in England who was St. Simon Stock and she gave him the little brown scapular. She promised that anyone wearing the scapular in devotion to the "Mother of God" would be saved. All Christians who honored "Our Lady of Mt. Carmel" and gave their devotion to her and the church would be saved. The church and the school were built around 1840. The original statue of "Our Lady of Mt. Carmel", was shipped here to our Little Italy in east Harlem NYC, from my mother's home town in Polla, Providence of Salerno, Italy. Many immigrants, who came from Polla, resided in the east Harlem area. It is one of the largest population of immigrants whomever migrated to that part of the city. The people lived, worked and brought up their children very proudly. Needless to say, our little area was very Italian. We all spoke different dialects, as our parents taught us. Funny cause while my parents taught me Italian, I taught the English. They picked up English way faster than I did Italian, but eventually I came to understand the language. But the people here worked hard and loved this country. Most of them never even returned home to see the family that they left behind in Europe. My parent left brothers and sisters and grandparents to try and make a better life for themselves here. Now we have multiplied to hundreds of cousins and today we are a 4th generation of "Medici" and "Amen". For those that were fortunate to have been born here, it was easy for them to work, because they spoke English. Many Italians were discriminated against in those days because they looked different and did not speak English. I am proud of my heritage and what they have contributed to the USA. We have all helped to make a difference.

East Harlem was a huge part of my life, although I have only expressed a few words about it. Sometimes it is hard trying to explain the area to individuals that did not work, attend school, or were raised in Harlem. If you were from Harlem, you immediately get it. Meeting someone from that area, built an automatic bond between you two, a sort of kinetic relationship to the neighborhood. One that I can't explain. Till this day when I meet a fellow "Harlemite", we seem to know each other and there is this strange feeling as if we are brothers and sisters. Maybe that's part of the reason why that area was called Pleasant Avenue. I have experience that great feeling to belong somewhere. Many people coming from the same town in Italy and having the same way of life from the old country, there was a bond we would have for a lifetime. But as the days of our youth were coming to a close, we all ventured on to different paths. Some married, some moved away, some kept in contact, and some lost touch of each other. East Harlem has now become Spanish Harlem. I am sure that there are memories that will still make us laugh and cry, when we think back and remember the days of our youth. Of course there were ups and there were downs, but through it all, I know that we all will have a bond that can never be broken. For those 25 blocks of East Harlem and Pleasant Avenue will always be a part of my family and me.

- From a little ole ... Harlem girl -

Why I Love Jazz

How did I become such a Jazz enthusiast? Strange? Being an Italian American woman, raised in the most talked about area, East Harlem, which is located between the East River Drive and Pleasant Avenue of New York City, aka The Little Italy of Harlem. Me? A lover of the Blues?

In my youth, growing up in East Harlem, was a very different experience than what you see today. It was a unique place to live. Thinking back to that time, the area was populated by Italians, some Irish and a few Germans. Being the curious person that I am, I wanted to know where the name Harlem came from. I worked for a wonderful Jewish man whose name was Mr. Alfred Biederman. He was a great inspiration to me, all the years that I worked for him. He was a very intelligent man, whom knew a lot of history about my area. Mr. Biederman, informed me all about East Harlem. "It was a Dutch and German community, in the 1700's", he told me, "The word Harlem resides from the Dutch", Mr. Biederman would say. I remember when there was horse racing on Pleasant Avenue, from East 116th street to 125th street. It was the most beautiful area, those 10 city blocks, which my eyes had ever beheld. The brownstone houses were only for professional people or wealthy people in the depression days. Most of them brownstones still exist today.

What does this have to do with my love of Jazz and the Soft Blues? Well, the unconquerable Harlem, west 125th street was the heart of Jazz and Blues. It was the place that elevated this genre which spoke to my soul, created melodies so beautiful that it sometimes didn't even need words. Revered as the starting point of black entertainment, which still exists today. New York City has the best shops in the world, and its fashion was unique. There was the Ritz shop and Smalls, there are night clubs, movies theaters, the Cotton Club, the Apollo, the Paradise Club, people came from all over to just say they visited New York City or one of its main attractions. But I think mostly they came to hear the greatest music of all time, at least to me, the "Broadway of Harlem", that Jazz music. During the 40's and 50's, I would go downtown to 52nd St., to The Metropole Café, where all the great jazz musicians would play. Well some played there, others just hung out. Many of them though, became big names, emerged and went on to play at Carnegie Hall. I would also go down by Greenwich Village, where jazz and supper clubs were the hot spots in New York City. Musicians would play all night into the wee hours of the morning, to sooth your troubles away.

To this day I can still hear the instruments singing, and the musician's souls declaring through their music. I still love jazz, the songs, words, and the sounds that come from this music; it is not like any other. It is in a world of its own! You don't listen to it, one must feel the music in order to understand the meaning of the jazz and blues. Being a romantic who enjoys all kinds of music, when I am down, depressed and my emotions prevail, the blues is what I go to for a pick me up, to feel on high again! Seems like I leave all my woes behind, when I listen to jazz. The instruments talk to you, my favorite being the piano was able to change my mood upon press of a key, the tenor saxophone mellowed me with every breath exhale, and the guitar would pluck every single care from my day away. For my childhood sweetheart it was the classical music of the violin playing the record of "Scherezade", "if music be the food of love then play on". Two of my brothers, John and Charles also loved this music... Jazz. I guess it is part of our heritage. During our youth this is the music we grew up on. The sound stereotypically designated to be just for a small population of Americans, wasn't so, because it resonated with my soul. A music that speaks to all, you just need to be human and capable of feeling the music. For we all have the same, feelings, thoughts, emotions and Jazz, and the Blues, tells us just that! So my love for it allows me to still play on. I came from the home of Jazz, which is Harlem... and for that I am grateful.

A Tribute to My Friends and Family

Mothers Sad Blue Eyes

My mother's eyes were blue, true and sad
They were like old souls from ancient times, which existed long
ago to the unknown
Her name was Maria Rose Amen
A tiny bit of a woman
Pale soft white skin, auburn hair, which sometimes turned
reddish or brown
She was like a flower that blooms in spring
Her beauty was no match to her kin
First born to be a queen
Only her destiny became her fate
The lord gave her many burdens to bear
Life took her youth to be a mother
Never complaining nonetheless
What was her passion in life?
I never knew...
Her sad eyes never told me so
America was her dream I believe
She left her country Italy
Never to return
Her love of music was Napolitano ballads of home
She always loved "Return to Sorrento" and Ballads of "Naples
and the Mediterranean sea"
She talked many times of her home town
With much sadness in the land of her youth
Along with the love of music she also danced to the tarantella
Death took her first love and she remained with a son alone and
abandoned again
She went on with prayers and hope always...
With her smiles and her sad blue eyes

Struggling, coping to survive, with all her strength,
determination and always believing in her heart all will be well
My mother's sad eyes always left me tearful
I never saw her cry
Buy maybe she did alone

Time Vanishes Like a Rose

Her love for her church and our Lady of Mt. Carmel was her
salvation
Praying to the saints and her devotion to St. Anthony gave her
strength
Her second love comes along with hope and happiness
Only to vanish into the night
Now her life was the savior of our brew
Her burden as a mother of six during depression days
Her life was working, working, with sadness
But always smiling never complaining to a soul with her sad blue
eyes
Maybe it's just a mother's way to comfort her children
She was given all the hardships that one can endure
War, depression days, worry, worry
All the time she fought to keep the brew safe and not abandon
her family
We did survive with all our ups and downs
Did we think about mom and her sadness?
I don't think so then, we were busy growing up never knowing
about our mom, her strife and struggles with loneliness
Mom was a giant
Although not an educated woman of the world
Her wisdom was that of the 20th century lady
Always with a smile and a wave of hand
She would say,
'DON'T WORRY ABOUT IT!'
Even when she wasn't speaking words
Only now, I remember how...
Her blue eyes could tell you that!
My mom did her part as the savior,
Nurturing, faithful and strong
She was far superior to the world
But never prostrated herself above it
Never even complaining when it wasn't right
With her ...
"Sad Blue Eyes"

- I know god has made a safe and beautiful place for you mom

A Tribute to My Friends and Family

in heaven-

I miss you mom!

Your daughter.

Time Vanishes Like a Rose

My Brother Charles Muro

I prayed for you every day Charles...
Heaven is where I know you long to wonder
To me, you were always the bright star
From the blue misty sky you painted the oceans and skies, with
such splendid colors
You were like a van Gough painting
Vibrant and beautiful

Charles, did you not know that you were so talented?
Your music, harmonica, dancing
You took anything apart/ in a jiff, and then were able to put it
back together again
I use to wonder, where did you come from?
"Muro" was an Italian artist
"Amen" your mother's name
So be it your ancestors derived from fame
You left us too soon on earth
You were always looking for that place
Beyond the horizon
That no one ever understood
Time on earth was not for you

My dear brother Charlie
If only you could feel or know what is in my heart
How much you meant to me
The pain I always felt for you, in my life time
My big brother who loved me
 I know that
You wheeled me around in my baby carriage
You always cared for me in a tender and gentle way
No one can imagine your thoughts
From the day you came to be
You were born out of love, from your Mom and dad, who loved
you dearly
Destiny changed your life
I know you always felt abandoned by it all

A Tribute to My Friends and Family

You had to leave your family while in your youth
To live alone in a strange faraway place, due to your ill health
Mother crying for her firstborn son
Never to have your mom near
The years were very sad for all us at home
How tragic it must have been for you
The unfortunate son, who always thought we never loved you
You always thinking you came from afar
Never belonged to our brew
It must have pierced your heart many times
Lack of understanding by us, not to know who you really were
I know that you are in heaven
And it's where you wanted to be all your lifetime
Your time on earth was not for you
And I pray that you are happy to be with all those beautiful
bright stars and painted skies
My dear brother Charlie
Look down on us remaining, and remember you were loved by
us all
But...
You were very loved by me

Your loving sister.

My Brother John A. Amen Medici

How can I explain my brother John? Does one know the meaning of John? One of the Apostles, Johnny Pump, Johnny Come Lately, John Bull the "Typical Englishman", John Doe the Unknown, Jonny… a hospital gown, the John… "Toilet" or slang for a pimp. But I know my baby brother, Johnny. He was conceived and born on a cold day in January. On a day when the freezing frost swallowed the sun and all its rays. John was born on our mom and pop's old fashioned Bedroom set. It was a dark and gloomy weird set of wood trimmings. Our family photos of grandma and grandpa hung above the walls of the bedroom. Oh, and don't forget Saint Anthony! That statue would look at you all day. We didn't know our grandparents. They had died before we were born, but we were taught about them and we were raised to respect them anyway, even if they were just pictures on the wall. The place of our childhood! We lived at 429 E.114 St. NYC (East Harlem), where our cold water flat was heated by a pot belly coal stove, no coal… you froze or went hungry. We had to carry our coal and wood up and down three flights of stairs to warm our bodies and keep our souls. Our apartment was on the 3rd floor, apt #7. The view from our living room window faced the beautiful Jefferson Park. When you wanted to escape reality momentarily we use the "Fire Escape", as we called them. Sitting out there was our getaway, our relaxation, our window to the world. Escape's view faced the East River, where we had swimming pools, parks with swings, soccer fields, and many more sports. Those were the days. It was good times in those days. Remember, our sun-bathing on the roof top, which was our beach! There we would cool ourselves on hot summer days and relax. Our feet were marked with Tar. Did we care? Not at all! We were too busy dreaming of real beaches and faraway places. On cold days the beach was closed, so we would stare at the bare trees, from our windows, waiting for spring to bear their leaves. Oh, how I remember John? As a baby, John had a beautiful face, he was a cuddly baby. His dark hair, brown eyes, and olive soft skin, made him resembled an Italian Cherub. John was almost lost to us at birth! Blue baby they called him, because he came out bluer than a blueberry. At birth he wasn't getting enough air to his lungs. But, thank God he survived. A lack of air didn't stop him at birth or growing up as a kid, John always had plenty to say, still till this day! There were many names for my baby brother through the years: Marble Head, Johnny Cake, Alter Boy, the Cry Baby, and Bookworm because he read everything in sight, and more. Johnny would be moaning, complaining, and talking all the time. It drove us crazy! But he was special... gifted. He was very bright, quick witted, a music lover, almost a monk if you would you believe that, an actor, business man, etc. But John was an enigma. I guess being born from Italian immigrant parents, with a mixture of Jewish and Middle Eastern decent, and of course can't forget the American/Italian Culture. Confusing? I guess he thought so, as well as we did. Our mother's maiden name was, "Amen", I guess that's what helped us get through.

Me being a middle girl child, when two baby brothers came, my role became being their care taker. I wasn't angry or jealous though. I would do anything to help my mother and our family. So, I didn't complain. Plus, I loved them like they were my own children. While other kids were playing and having fun, I was bathing John and George, dressing them, changing diapers, feeding them and singing them to sleep. I was too busy to be a teenager. My thoughts of love, romance and boys had to take a back seat. My friends wondered about me, I wanted to play with them and to grow up so to speak, but I had responsibilities. They didn't have brothers or sisters to care for, or diapers to change. Ok, maybe I was a little bitter. Picture me as a young tot, trying to be a mom! I didn't laugh then, but now I do, I still crack up to this day. Maybe my role was to be the mom then, for I never became a mom later on in my life. Now, you boys are all grown up. You guys must have hated me at times. What did I know about motherhood? I still a kid too! I wanted to play just like you guys. So your play time became my play time. Our afterschool activities consisted of fun at "The Playground". Off to Jefferson playground me, John and George would go every day. Where I went, you went. We would swing, play ball, swim, etc. Sometimes we would even skip off to the movies. Was I a good babysitter? Who knows? Occasionally, there were falls off swings, bruises all over, busted lips, bumps on head, you guys getting lost in the park, cars crashing, a few broken bones. I ran from it all, or denied my involvement. There was many days that I was too frightened to go home. I didn't want mom to cry or be mad at me. Poor George's leg. A little secret is that I cried almost all the time, just to myself, all alone. You both would get lost all the time. Guess you both were hiding from me?

A dear friend of mine, Benjamin, was my savior, he had a great influence in my life. Ben was always there for me! Growing up in an awesome era, caring for my two baby brothers, John and George, would have been extremely difficult having no friends and feeling overwhelm. Benjamin helped me keep my sanity. While my other friends were annoyed at the two of you having to tag-along, Benjamin was always was there to help me keep an eye of you two. But what an adventurous childhood, we three had! What kind of influence did I have on you? Was it good? I do hope so! Do you remember these things from our childhood? Do you remember the park attendant, John Halbin? My first secret puppy love! Blue eyes, blond curly hair, he was a handsome prince. Remember how he used to act like he was our older brother? What do you think about now John, now that you are all grown up? Time has been good to us. With all its terror, laughter, sadness, and the fear of the unknown, when all our experiences unfold, and the facts of life are told, looking back on the paths that we chose... I would say, God has been good to you and our family.

Working hard on one's self is a tremendous feat. If we dig down deep into our souls we will become aware. Then we will be able to laugh or cry any sorrow away! You have accomplished many things in your life time, most of all, being blessed with dear Marsha, and two lovely girls Marisa and Corrine.

A Tribute to My Friends and Family

How well would you say that I describe my brother Johnny Cake? We bonded a very long time ago, looking back and realizing it today... I happy that you were always there, as my brother, sometimes a mentor, and friend! Hoping you will always remember our strange relationship. We are growing up, getting older and wiser. Forever compassionate, understanding and most of all WITH LOVE,

Your loving sister!

Time Vanishes Like a Rose

My Brother Frank Medici

I remember my brother Frank so well. As the older brother he took care of me from infantry throughout my teenage years. Our father, before I was born, was married to Josephine Priore, Franks mother, who died and left our father John Medici a widower when Frank was two years old. They were from Italy, even though Frank was born in New York City. You see Frank is my half-brother, even though in my family we never used the term, for we all loved each other dearly. At around three or four years of age, he was sent to Italy to live with his grandmother and grandfather. Frank loved his grandparents and he really enjoyed their company. He used to always tell me how they treated him like royalty. In I believe that in those days in was very hard to have a family and survive, without having a spouse. There were many hardships and challenges of being a single parent, even more so than nowadays. After a few years of being on his own, John Medici married again. He married my mother, a woman named Rose Amen, whom at the time also had a son, called Charles Muro. They were both widowers at the time. They were matched together by mutual friends that they had from Harlem. Therefore, when I was born, I now had two older brothers, both of whom were my "Half-brothers", both born in the same year, 1923. I loved them both dearly; they always took care of me as a child. We became a family of six siblings, my two older brothers, Frank and Charles, my sister Ann and I, and then John and George whom were born 10 years later than myself.

What I can remember about Frank the most is that he was wild and uncontrollable. Referred to as "Street Smart", because he liked to rip and run the streets of Harlem, learning from its wilds and ways. Frank was the usual teenager he loved to dance, play sports, and run around with his friends from Harlem. They were not really bad kids and never hurt anyone. They just upset the family while doing so many crazy antics, which to them was letting out steam. He had a nickname: "Hot Dog". To me that was awful! But he did not mind as many of his friends had awful nicknames too: Mushy Callaghan, The Zip, The General, Red, Chippy, Goloeo, Beans, Pigion Toes, Goose, The Lawyer and many more. So many episodes came from this brew. Episodes that may seem funny, but were not so funny to the family when they occurred. Like the time that Frank and his friends decided to go to California. Seems normal and innocent, but the only issue is that they decided to bike there and without my or their parents knowledge. Frank was missing for a while and my mom started to worry about him. In the middle of the night there was a knock on the door and I heard a police officer talking to my poor mom whom was so frightened. It seem that they were picked up by the policeman somewhere in Brooklyn, and told him that they were heading to California. At that time, I was very young so I could not grasp the whole meaning as to what was going on! I know my mom was happy to see Frank and that he was ok, my father, I don't remember if he was angry with him or not but I would guess he was! That was only one of the many. Frank and his friends were picked up and held in a holding place somewhere in West 125th street. It must have been a jail, "The Tombs". Crime? The police accused them of stealing shoes from one of the neighborhood shoe store. They denied it, and would still be denying it down to this day. Well another disaster and of course my mom always defended Frank. She always did, and still would be down to this day. I remember going to see Frank in this place, which was not so nice of a place to be. It wasn't a pleasant site to see. My poor brother, whom I looked up to in so many ways, was down and out. We brought him food to eat, for Frank was locked up again. I tried to cheer him up. He was extremely happy to see us, especially my mom. My mom had to see the congressmen in the area to help her get Frank out of jail. She did not have any money for lawyers so that is what many people did in those depression days. We did get Frank out and he came home with us. He told mom that he did not steal anything and she believed him. She loved him very much and would always try and do all she could for Frank, she had his best interest at heart. But my mother was conflicted, as much as she loved him, he kept getting into trouble. What was best for him? She always defended him. My pop was strict and he did not take too much interest in Frank not because he did not care, but because he had so many of his own demons and he viewed Frank as being problematic. I believe that my father did argue with my mom many times over Frank and Charles. I think there were some comparisons made between Charles and Frank. Whereas, Charles was a quiet boy, he loved to paint, loved music, could build things with no problem, but his asthma limited his education, for he could not attend school, Frank was wild! Therefore, there was a lot of tension about my two brothers at times between my parents. However, from what I can remember the boys did get along well with each other. Charles was a sickly boy with bad asthma, and Frank was wild!

Anyway, there were a lot of troubling things happening in the streets of Harlem at those times. Ethnic wars, fights and battles. Crooked and abusive policemen. Trying times. And guess who was always dead smack in the middle of it? It was my mom who made this decision about Frank going to, CCC Camp as it was called, Construction Conservatory Core Camp. The government provided this camp. It is there that Frank learned how to deal with life. It was either that or he would have to go to some sort of school. Nevertheless, Frank did not want to go to school so he had to attend this program or else! Today it's called (DEP). He worked on that city job for 30 years and eventually became a supervisor. He also held a 2nd job at night time in Bloomingdales department store on 59th st. There he worked for 30 years also and become a manager of that department store. He liked working there and was appreciated. I will admit I like it too, because I would get 50% off. That program made Frank a new man. He learned all about construction work, trimming trees, planting, cutting grass. This work was done in all the public parks and I must say he was very good at all this. I do believe it is from his father who was a construction worker and an army man and a tough one at that! Needless to say Frank, "Grew Up", so to speak. He started doing little odd jobs on the streets of Harlem, he got himself an old beat up truck, went all over picking up scraps of metal and old pieces of junk metal, which he would sell for money. He became a hard worker and loved what he was doing. He made money and was happy for a while.

During World War II, Frank joined the army. I guess you can say like father, like son in this regard. He was a good solider. He fought in Italy, France, and Germany. He never liked talking about the war when he got home. He served in the 5th Infantry and I know he saw a lot of action. I wrote to him as a teenager. Growing up during those hard times was tough on families. We worried about Frank all the time. Frank was the rock of the family. He endured a lot growing up with his half-brother Charles, they had a tough times, a lot of ups and downs with my pop who also had his bad times. He was lame in one of his legs from a construction accident. He never got over that! He used to be tall, handsome, vibrant and a first World War veteran. He too had his own demons. We all endured many hardships in our family. Frank got home unharmed after many years of service in the army. I remember him just wanting to sleep all the time. I guess he deserved it. At the time i didn't understand it. I would bug him, "get up, get up! What is wrong with you?". I never realized till today after seeing so many veterans doing the same that he must have been worn out from the war. War has an effect on a solider, that civilians just sometimes don't understand. Thankfully, he was able to cope with his life after coming home after the war to the best of his ability.

Frank was a great father, husband, and grandfather. One who was truly devoted to his family. His family was the most important thing in his life. After the war, frank married one of the most beautiful women i ever saw in my lifetime. My mom introduced them. Her name was Yolanda. They had been together for about 70 years. They had three beautiful children together, Josephine, John, and Patricia. My sister-in-law Yolanda was the most honorable mother, friend. She was gentle, with a loving heart. She brought so much beauty and respect to our family. I know our family all agreed to that she probably never had even spoken a harsh word about anyone in all those years together with frank. She was his soulmate and she loved him with all her heart. She left us right after frank passed. We all said she could not live without frank. They are both gone today but never forgotten! We still love you Frank and Yola!

Frank had a great personality. He was a good listener, and always tried to help people, advising them on what was best. He never got angry or shouted. He didn't have a mean bone in his body. He was intelligent, knew his politics and understood how the world worked. Frank saw it all. He lived his life. I was the baby sister you cared for! I loved you most of all frank! We had a strong bond together from the start of my childhood. My dear loving brother i wrote this letter for your 80th birthday and somehow i had to change my thoughts today. You are not here but the memories of my childhood still lingers with me today of your warmth and the love you shared with me. It is hard to sum up one's life in a few pages. There has been so much more to all our lives and our family regarding all the years we have spent together. You always will be the prince, as mom would say about her sons. She adored you boys with her saying "my son , my sons"! Frank you will always be a special brother, and friend. Oh, how i do hope that you are in a safe place. Remember you will never be forgotten by me. I love you dearly! I also believe we will all meet again somewhere in time.

And so remembering my brother frank...
I remember him always being there for me growing up. From my youth, through my teenage years and even as an adult. Listening to all my problems, telling me to smile and "not to worry about it". We had so many good times with you frank and our family. It was always at your house that we would celebrate the holidays. It was always wonderful to be together. As it is said, blood is thicker than water! Oh, how i miss those times. You were my brother. I, your baby sister, and we a family that special beyond compare.

My Baby Brother George Medici

I remember that cold day in January. Mom was in her bedroom, which is where you were conceived. She was waiting for the Mid Wife to appear to deliver her baby. In those days, there was no Ultrasound or doctors available. Therefore, we did not know if you were going to be a boy or girl. Midwives were used for delivery process. I was just a tot myself, not even fully aware of what was to happen. Thinking back, I am trying to remember all that was present, but I cannot recall. All I know is that it was awesome! I was told to leave the room and go to the neighbor's apartment and just wait, it was all strange to me. I was the baby girl in this family then! My Brother John was born two years before also in January. I waited and waited for what seemed like an eternity, but not before long there came this beautiful baby boy. What a great feat for mom and pop again, another baby boy! As I looked upon you, I thought, "Here is this baby, with skin so fair, eyes of brown, and blonde hair like an angel. You looked like a Prince! At first, many people could not believe where he came from! You didn't look like the usual baby of Italian Heritage with dark skin. Our cousins and aunts viewed you as this beautiful angel, they adored you! My pop was flying high. He was asked, "what do you want to name this beautiful baby boy?", being close to the month of February, he replied, "call him George, like George Washington"! In our family, we didn't have a "George". Growing up, George was a quiet boy. Even though, I was his sister, at times it felt like I was mom also. I had to change diapers, feed him, baby brother I looked after you day and night! It wasn't too difficult though, for you never cried and always did what you were told. George was so precious and you just wanted to kiss him all the time! And I did! At times you felt like my very own son.

George and John always wanted play in Jefferson Park. The park was located in East Harlem, from East 111th Street to East 114th Street. There were swings, a swimming pool, ball playing, the park had it all. We would always go there. They got lost in the park all the time, it was awful, I would be scared that

someone kidnapped them, and then they would just jump out of nowhere. Even though, I loved my brothers, you guys did preoccupy a lot of my time in my teenage years, I too wanted to have fun! But, I was playing mommy
and I never complained, I guess because of my love for you two. But, it was not all fun and games, tragedies did occur. For example, when George was around five or six years old, while I was watching him outside I lost track of where you went. Frantically, I called out your name. I guess you were scared yourself, and you ran into the street and were hit by a car. I thought that was the end of both our lives! You were taken to Roosevelt Hospital on Randall Island with a fractured leg. I thought that you were going to be left lame or something. The family was in quite an uproar about the situation. It turned out fine, George just had to have his leg in a cast for a few months, but he recovered with no problems. The whole ordeal was tough on me though. I was so upset at the time, thinking that I seriously hurt my brother that I ran away. Pop had told me not to come home jokingly, if he was going to be lame in any way and I took it serious. Wow. This was a really awful time for me! I was 15 years old, and that event still stays fresh in my mind even till this day. Well, time went on and George still hugged me all the time! I was not fired. Yes, I was still the babysitter and thank god for that!

Unfortunately, we all must grow up, and George did just that. He went from going to school, to working with mom for years in a glove factory. My mom kept George close to her all the time he was her prince and a knight in shining armor! He also was an all-around great athlete, he had a beautiful body, like an Adonis, fit for anything and every type of sport. The running joke was that George felt like he was Superman. As a teen George spent a lot of time out of the house, he was very popular and went from being quiet to being the leader of the pack so to speak. Suddenly, George signed up for army life, he was not drafted. I must say, "Like Father, like Son", seeing how my pop had also joined the army and was a soldier in World War I. He also signed up for the war in Italy. George was in the Cuba crisis, which was an alarming time in our country. We prayed that all would be well, and thank God it ended up to be. After George left the army, he married a woman named Diana. They were such a beautiful couple and they had two beautiful children. My brother George became the face of a man whom had many jobs. He was a very successful Insurance Broker, he held the position of a Post Office Worker, a Bus Matron for the city caring for disabled children, etc. He loved those kids and cared for them like they were his own. George was a man of many talents as well, one of those being art. He loved to paint, his work was like that of Van Gogh! Get back to your art! Don't let that talent go to waste my little brother. George and I are very close knitted, even though we are brother and sister, our relationship seems more like mother and son at times. It's amazing how things have changed over the years, I basically raised and watched over you, but as you grew into your own the tide had changed to you becoming my protector, there for me through the good and the bad. When we are together we seem to laugh all the time. We are so connected that everything that happens to me happens to him! Literally! When my tooth ached, so did his. I had sinus issues, George too. Gall bladder, George as well. I always joked with him that it is just in our "Genes".

As a grown man today, George is remarried to Ann Theresa. Now, these are two peas in a pod. I am happy for them both and wish them all the best that life has to offer. As I, recall our relationship over the years, I just want you to know that I love you. You have meant so much to me, and continue to and time goes on. Even though, this is only part of our story, there were many more difficulties. We all survived today because family is what life is all about. This is not the end of our story. Life definitely has much more is store for us. My dear baby brother, enjoy life and make every moment count. Wishing you love and peace always. I do hope you will always have the wind beneath your wings. And don't forget! I took care of you ……… with all my love and understanding!
Your Sister!

Sister's True Story: A Child's Lost Love

I was playing tennis one day with my friend Pat. We played Tennis in the Bronx often many times during the summer months. One day, Pat and I were talking about our youth and where we lived growing up as children. Pat and I have been friends for the last ten years and we never talked too much about ourselves, especially not about the times before we knew each other. To both of our amazement, when I mentioned the place where I was born and the street address where I lived as a child. Pat told me that he also lived in the same apartment complex. I said, " Pat that is impossible! I do not remember you or your family! ". He stated that his two older sisters would remember this incident, and he was going to ask them about it! I thought that Pat was pulling my leg, but we continued talking and now started to get into more details. He went on to tell me a story about his first love as a child, and that how he had never gotten over this little girl, that he fell in love with, and never forgot her! I thought that was strange, how could you at the age of 6 fall in love first of all, second, you are 73 and still think about her. "How could you even remember that far back", I chuckled in my mind. But, he was got so excited about the story that I didn't want to tease him. I asked him to tell me more about his memories of his childhood. He said that all his life he thought about this little blonde haired, fair skin and green eyed pretty face girl! As children they played together in the apartment complex. In those days, kids did that very often. We were not allowed to venture into the streets like children today! One thing I was sure of is that this girl, Pat's first love, was not me! But I thought that it was sweet that even after all these years, he held onto her in his memory. I told him that I have a sister whose name is Antoinette, then I told him about another girl in another apartment house down the street who was also called Antoinette, she was our cousin and she looked very much like my sister. Our family heritage, is known to name all the firstborn girls Antoinette! At this time I was just trying to see if any of those names rang a bell to him. Pat said, "No, she lived in my apartment complex. And they called her DuNette"!

Wow, now I was sure he was telling the truth, it's an Italian nick name for Antoinette. So

I went on to ask him, "what apartment house did you live in?". He replied, "In 429 East 114 St. NYC on the first floor". Now, I was really going crazy with all this, I could not believe where this was going. I said Pat, that is where I lived also, but I don't remember you at all. We lived on the 3rd floor. In the meantime we went on talking about this little girl that broke his heart!

Pat was going on and on about his first love. He also said that she told him she didn't like him, Pat said he was hurt! Then Pat told me about a detail that he remembered about this little girl, he said "she had a bad sunburn on her shoulders and on her back, she use to have to wear some white cream on her skin for protection. She also would wear this shirt that covered her shoulders"! Pat had just described to me my sister. My sister Antoinette could never take any sun not even today. I was positive that it was my sister that Pat fell in Love with at the age of 6. She had always been a Tom Boy or labeled as a bit of a tough girl. Wow! I laughed so hard, and then told Pat, "Yup that's my sister alright". Then together we laughed so hard. Life was throwing some curves at Pat and me that day! We departed from each other and when I saw him the next day, I had returned with a photograph of the two of us, me and my sister at the age of 5 or 6 years of age. As sure as this story is true, he picked my sister Antoinette, right out of the photo. He said that was his Antoinette! And how he had never forgotten about her. "Where is she, what is she doing nowadays?", he asked. You know that I had to arrange a meeting with the two of them! I told him she lived here in the Bronx, and was well, and married with a wonderful family. He wanted to see her so badly, so I told him that I would try to arrange a meet if it was ok with her. The next day, I talked to my sister and told her all about Pat. I asked if it was ok to give him her phone number! I then told my sister of how the story unfolded. Ann laughed so hard, and told me that she could not remember him or the incident! The sun poisoning was a true story, but a Pat did not ring an alarm to her. So told me that it was ok, and so I gave him the phone number, and they made arrangements to meet in Pelham Bay Park one day. Ann asked Pat, "How would I know who you are?", Pat replied that he would have a red rose, and for her to bring a red balloon. Isn't this romantic?! When they got together, they started talking about their childhood. Pat told her that he often thought of their time together as children, how he remembered her sun poisoning and how she didn't like him! He recalled this one time when they were together, how he wanted to kiss her, but she told him that she did not like him! They went on to talk about their lives. Pat was getting married again, he was living in Florida, and was very happy. He comes back to New York on occasions to see his children who were lives in the Bronx and to play some tennis with his family and friends. My sister told me they got along fine and that he wanted to keep up their friendship. Antoinette said, of course, and she told him that her husband knew about the meeting that took place and recalled their childhood events from the past. Guess what? This does not stop here! The world is a very small place. Pat asked her who her husband was and where did he come from, she told him he also lived in the Bronx, and this her name by marriage was Curto, Antoinette Curto. "What is your husbands first name?", Pat asked. "Where did he go to school?", he continued. Antoinette, told him his name was Danny Curto. Pat in awe blurted out, "I know him. We went to high school together. We were buddies." Life is very strange and wonderful at times. We don't know who and when we will meet someone from our past life. They all got together and went out for some beers and talked about their childhood memories. What an awesome encounter this was that day! I will never forget that memory. They all exchanged phone numbers, and were to meet again, on his return from Florida.

We are so connected to one another in many ways. Who knows how the people we encounter in our everyday life with thoughts of yesterday and tomorrow, how they can touch our hearts forever.
The search was over for Pat and his first love for "DuNette" aka

A Tribute to My Friends and Family

Antoinette.

On August 22, 2003, I received a call from one of Pat's friends from Florida, and they said Pat, passed away suddenly! We were all in shock and felt so sad about losing a wonderful man who was such a loving, tender, gentle person. How he could leave us so suddenly? To this day it still amazes me and puts a smile on my face, I can't imagine how anyone else could ever remember that blonde haired, fair skin, green-eyed girl with a pretty face, but Pat did and after decades of searching for that first love as a child he found her! Ann and I attended a Memorial for Pat here in the Bronx, and she got to see his two sisters and many of Pat's friends from Pelham Bay Park who attended the Memorial that day. It's a somewhat sad story but true! As a note: The balloon went to Pat's Granddaughter and Ann went home with The Rose!

The Lost Piano

This is a sad story about my recollection of a beautiful piano that existed in my family's apartment a long time ago. My family lived in a cold water flat located in East Harlem. For anyone who does not know what a cold water flat is, I will explain as best as I can. It is a three story building that has three floors. On each floor, there are two apartments. We had neighbors next door to each other. Unbelievably we all got along fine. There was one bathroom located on each floor, so each family used the same john! Not so fun when you think about it, but we all took turns using and cleaning the bathroom. All the rooms in each apartment ran like a railroad, one after the other. So our kitchen was the first room, then the bedrooms, until you came to the last room which was our parlor, or living room. Whichever you wanted to call it! That is where we listened to the radio, watched tv, and had our family gatherings.

That room faced Jefferson Park. Sundays were football and soccer games. Just kids playing on the field, but this were a big treat for us.

Those were the depression days, so we all had to conserve all we could and work very hard to exist. My parents were immigrants from Italy, and it was a difficult time in our lives, especially with a family with six children. My parents did not speak much English. They were learning though as hard as they could. We all were teaching them the English language. We learned to speak Italian and they learned to speak English from us children. We struggled, but we did eat well, went to school, did our house chores, and helped the best way we knew how! Family life was dear to all of us. This was taught to us, to respect others and our family. That was the main key to our way of life. In those days, we had to respect our mother and father, but it did not stop there we also had respect for all our cousins, aunts, our parents friends, etc. We did not have a choice, like it or not! We never questioned our parents; they were not mean or strict, but we had to obey their rules. This was what they were taught in Italy from their generation and it was going to continue down to our generation in America. There was not much work for immigrants. It was a great feat to just endure. If you were fortunate enough to have a city job, then you were considered rich in those days! My mom was an angel from heaven. She held us together in the worst times of our lives. She worked as a seamstress and pop was a construction worker, making good money. All was well for a while until the crazy day when my pop was in an accident that left him lame in one leg. Pop was out of work for a long time. He was not able to work in that field again and mom had all the responsibility for the six of us.

Well let's get to the piano! You might say what does all this has to do with a piano. We were not rich by any means, but, to have a piano in your parlor was a great opportunity for someone during the time of war and the depression days. I am a lover of music! Some of my favorite music was that of the big bands, opera, jazz, classical, and doo wop. Music is the way of expressing oneself. My creed has always been, "If music be the food of love, then play on". I was about 5 or 6 years old when we got the piano. I think my mom had purchased the piano, but it is possible that someone did not want it any longer and gave it to us. I don't have that information. What I do know is that we lived on the third floor and we had to get this piano up to our apartment. There was no way it could come up three flights of stairs. There was a back door that led to the hallway this door was an emergency door. Every apartment in the tenement had the same door located in the parlor. So it was brought up through the window located in the parlor room. The window had to be broken out of the frame, so that we could get it into the room. The piano was made of dark wood and it was a stand up piano roll with all 88 keys. It was a beautiful piano I thought. All the kids were extremely excited about having a piano in the house. We use to play it with our feet and when the music came off the roll, it made music to us. At that time all I could think of is how wonderful it was to have that instrument in our apartment. We always had a radio, record player, or some sort of music in the apartment, but this piano took the cake. I know my mom always tried to have the newest items and keep up modern times she was so ahead of her time, a real 20th century lady. Some of the most memorable times that I had were sitting there with my brothers, playing the piano and hearing music from this beautiful big dark instrument! My older brothers Frank and Charles knew more about the piano than I did. Charles really had good musical ability. With all my love for music you probably would have thought that the better player would have been me. The tunes for the instrument kept us sane for some time.

I never remembered what truly happened to that piano. It seems that either it was not working any longer, or as I heard the story, my father tore it up into small pieces of wood and used it for fire wood into the pot belly stove to help warm up the apartment. Did the music go out the window into the pot belly stove? If so, that is strange to me. My pop loved music. He listened to Opera on *WQXR* every Saturday with me at 2pm. Was it because my mother wanted that piano for Charles? It may be that pop did not want him to have the piano! I don't know! All I know is that there was a piano in my life, and that it was located in the living room.

In my older years, I still often think of the piano. Why we had one, and why did it leave us? I always wanted to play the piano. I sometimes tell this story to friends and I laugh about it. What we had to go through in order to get the piano up into the third story of a tenement building, tearing a window out of its frame, and then to leave in pieces, I'll never know why it left us in that way! Who knows if it didn't, maybe I'd be a famous pianist.

My Nephew: The Phantom

We never say too much about, our nieces and nephews! To say the least, Steven was my nephew, God's child, my friend, and more! Born to my only Sister Ann Medici Galiardo. The first grandson and first Nephew of our family. He wasn't like many other young boys growing up, he was unique, and he was special. His Blue eyes were like stars from the heavens! He had fair skin so soft like the wings of an angel. The day that he was born, I held him in my arms so tight. I was afraid to let go! I thought about how fast you would grow, how one day you would wander, and be in a rush to be a man. Remembering Steven, one would never forget that he was a gentle soul, kind, loyal and humorous. That Clef in his chin was like a smile. How his smile warmed your heart. My first nephew meant so much to me! I became a first time aunt, and I have never been a mom! I borrowed Steven from my sister as times, he became like my son. We were like the best of friends. We laughed, and cried together. Reaching the prime of his life, he was still like that small boy I knew. He was there for me, cared for me, always the helpful Soul, running errands, picking me up, shopping, my handy repair man, he never said no. Most of all, when I was down and out, the phone would ring, "Hello Theresa, how are you today?". You will never know how much that made my day! Was Steven spoiled? I wouldn't say so, even though no one could ever say no to those blue eyes. "Don't leave the block", his Mom would say, and he obeyed. He was a silent, coy, shy and quite somber boy. He became a Con-Ed man, and a faithful father to his three lovely girls, whom he could not say no to. No matter what the strain would be, he never complained and would just try to make them happy. I admired him for that. Now I am thinking back and trying to sum up one's life and meaning to the world in a brief moment, and it's difficult but I will try. Steven, your name means "CROWN". St. Stephen was stoned to death, by the Jews, he was the first martyr and mentioned every day in individual's prayers. He was a "Cannon of the Mass", buried in Rome, born on the day after the "Birth of our Lord". December 26, is your named day.

Therefore, you are blessed, so don't fret the small stuff. Oh Dear Steven, with your blessings, you continue to be a blessing to others, doing more than your share to make your loved ones happy. You have touched my heart, again and again! I must say, you have also left a spark in all the corners of our family as well. At times we thought, you were there, but behold you were gone. The Phantom is your name, or game. It's no joke, to escape! And you did! You are loved by all, so do not stray! Just try to stay close to our hearts. My friend and dear nephew, be happy, I'll love you always. You left us too soon, in June. Now we pray that you are looking down on us smiling, while the memory of you forever remains in our hearts!

You're Loving Aunt,

A Tribute to My Friends and Family

Smiling Ann Theresa: My Sister-In-Law

To my friend, my confidant, sister In-law, and the forever smiling Ann Theresa. Where do I start in trying to explain Ann Theresa? We met so long ago on Morris Park Avenue, in the Bronx. Our apartments were right next to one another. We bonded at once. It was the start of a long lasting friendship. Ann Theresa had that tall striking look, beautiful green eyes that shone like emeralds from faraway places, so rare! Her curly dark hair would constantly change like the flowers of the field, it was brown, sometimes red, but now a beautiful grey. She was called, "Sophia Loren" of the Bronx! We meshed like two peas in a pod! We were part of a wonderful crazy crew too! My mind still recalls the memories of: Maryann, Helen, Marilyn, Andrea, Rena, and Crazy Jo Ann (crazy but lovable). Everyone loved Ann Theresa. She was always full of constant laughter, smiles, sincerity, and humor. She was a great friend, above all remembered for her smiles! Remember, Castle Hill Pool? Sally's Hi Tide? Sal, the owner? Sal was a charmer. All the women loved him. He was generous, had a great personality and easy on the eyes. Remember how us girls were known as, " The Queens of Castle Hill Pool"! We never really ventured into the water, "look out my hair", but we were bikini beauties. I must say, we all looked really great. All of Castle Hill pool patrons looked on in Awe! You just had to Love them! I did! Remember, "The Cappuccino Coffee" from the Venice Bar and Restaurant located on Morris Park Avenue? No one made it like Mike the bartender. It was our best kept secret! It also had the greatest tasting food in the Bronx! Oh, how we had spent many nights together there at the Venice. There was fun, laughter, and sadness too. We girls had our ups and downs. We also had our little secrets! It's what girls do! Ah! Do men understand that? NO! What are friends for? But to chat a bit about life! About our wants, desires, and dreams. We achieve some, but not all. Life is so full of wonders, that we really never know what lies ahead of us, or what paths we may follow.

When Ann Theresa first came into my life she was married to

Time Vanishes Like a Rose

Frank Moran. Frank Moran was a very loving man, warm and generous, always trying to achieve the highest goals in life. They had two beautiful children, Laura Ann and Lawrence. Do you know why both children are named with the initials L? Because they were full of love and laughter! Isn't that amazing? We were all friends. Remembering Frank, I think about how he Italian food, and espresso coffee. Oh, how we had shared many good times together. He would be so proud of his two children today! Pray for us Frank! Who would of thought that after his passing we would actually become family? I mean you had to marry my brother George to do so but I guess, it wasn't so bad. Dear Ann Theresa, you have come a long way. From all your Yesterdays, now it's your tomorrow! It's your day! Your love story is truly a wonder. Pure destiny. We dreamt sometimes for untouchable desires. Did you ever think that your life would turn out like it did? 25 five years ago you met, George Medici. Never knowing what faith had in store for the both of you. George with his family, and you had your family, everything merged so well and your kids mingled together as friends. You both had your secret desires, from the past. Ann Theresa, you always were in awe of George! You both are a great pair, I must say, two souls entwined together as one. Ann Theresa Smiling and George happy as a lark, that he had Ann Theresa by his side. You have come into our Medici Family bring happiness and laughter to us all. I am happy to express how proud I am to have you with us and I know the whole family feels the same. You brighten up our table with your smiles, oh how we cherish you. Through the good times, and bad days, you have always been there as stood tall as family. Be happy with my baby brother George! May God bless you both now and for the many wonderful
years to come!

Keep Smiling! My Dear Friend!

My Last Dance with My Father

All the years growing up with papa, I always wondered, who was he? I mean, yes he was my father but, what made him tick? What kind of person was he growing up as a kid? I always yearned to know! Remembering back when I was a little girl about 5 or 6 years old of age, I remember desiring to for my papa to pick me up and hold on to me with affection. That time never came. At least not to my recollection. It was strange to me, he was vague, but at that age how can any child fully know or understand anything! That didn't stop my admiration of him. My father was one of the most handsome, vibrant, strong and funny guys that I ever met. Papa was an immigrant from a faraway place in Italy. In the later years of my life, I have had the good fortunate of traveling to Italy in search for my family's heritage. I desperately wanted to know why they came to America and how they lived while in Italy. In Italy my papa was a daredevil, he was a policeman, and he even volunteered into the army and joined the guerrilla warfare. It was a tough part of the Army and he did see some action in WWI. John my papa, was the talk of Italy in his youth. Born 9/1/1897, he was the youngest of 11 children. It had to be difficult trying to divide love amongst all these children. Did my father yearn for affection from his parents the same as I did from him? Grandma Medici was a very tough lady as I was told! My father was always roaming in Italy looking for adventure and he did find it in his own way! In America, papa use to tell us stories all the time, about his adventures. We had always laughed and thought that he made them up in between few glasses of red wine. We loved his stories though! In one story is he was on guard, and by mistake he shot his own captain! So many years went by and we had to respect Pop no matter what he did or said. That was a strong hold in our family. Papa never expressed his thoughts or feelings to anyone, I am sure he had many demons of his own, but I'll never know! His love for music amazed me for he would listen to the radio and above all things, he would listen to the Operas. So I too listened with him. He would tell me all these fascinating stories of the Opera in Italy.

Time Vanishes Like a Rose

Today I am an Opera Lover, thanks to my papa. I believe that my papa left me with that kind of love. In America, papa was a construction worker. He always said that he helped build some of the bridges and roads that we would use daily. We were always told that Italians built this country. History does state those facts. As a kid, I believed that it was my papa. Not all the years with papa were the best of times. When I was young, my father was in an accident on the job that left him lame in one leg, so he walked with a limp. This was in the time of the depression, and he did not work for some time because he could not walk for a long time. This was the worst times for my father, a man of iron, he was never the same man. I remember. He was not able to walk, dance, or work for a very long time. So had an even bigger effect on the person he was, making him a little unpleasant. He drank too much and had a lot of anger inside of him all the time. He became a different father in my eyes! His pride would never allow him to think of getting help as well, that was a no no in those days. I believe his soul was tormented, comparing and contrasting the man he was in Italy to the man he became in America, especially because of the accident! After a while, he became a chef and worked in various places in NYC and the Bronx. I must say that he was good at his job! Many times I do remember how he wanted to cook at home and my mom would say, "NO Way!". I don't know why, seems he was pretty good at it. I think this job help him get some of his confidence back. My papa was not a mean man to any of his children, but he and mom did have a little tension between them. I chalk it up to parents arguing over the trials and tribulations of life. He showed his affections in different ways to all his children, through telling us stories, sharing of music and through his extreme sense of humor. These seemed to come easier for him than outward showy displays of affection. He was a somber man. It was difficult trying to guess what was in his heart or of what he was thinking about at times. His silence always made me wonder what it was that he was pondering about, but then he would teach me about the most beautiful words from many Operas. I just learned to accept it, that was the way he was. I assumed that

my papa's parents too had a tough time showing love. Eleven children? How does two people divide up themselves to supply love equally to them all? That would be quite a feat! What existed in the 1800s with his parents growing up most likely impacted the man he was today. But I loved my papa! Even though there was drama in our household growing up, I know I am the person that I am today because of him, my mother, and Jesus, who was always there for me. Encouraging me always to "forgive your demons", which I did! To me you will always be my strong, handsome devil, who was unfortunate and misunderstood. A man who tried to do all the rights things in his life. I will always remember our last dance, Papa …
It was on my wedding day! Loving memories that will never vanish with time.

From your daughter lovingly… Theresa Dolores Medici

A Loving Son's Letter to His Mother

When I was about to enter the sixth grade in New York City I was having a great time hanging out on the street with the local kids. My mother abruptly abducted all of us kids to a foreign land 50 miles upstate, which, by the way deprived me of participating in the "Midnight Basketball" program soon to come. The place we moved to was a farm situated on 12 1/2 acres of land in a place called Putnam Valley. Mom thought it would be a good idea if I learned to milk a cow, so we went to an old farmer, Mr. Papp, and I learned to milk. I hadn't even seen a cow before, milk came in bottles. It wasn't long before Mom came home with a cow she had purchased at a livestock auction. I had to get up so early to milk this cow that the chickens weren't even awake yet. And if I decided not to milk the cow it would probably have died from a ruptured udder, subjecting me to cowicide, as nobody else knew how to milk, or even showed an interest in learning. Then after school I had to milk the cow for a second time every day. Not only was I forced into this work but you can only imagine the mess a cow makes being in a barn all night consuming oats, hay and water. There were hundreds of pounds of this stuff to deal with before I could even begin to milk. As if this wasn't enough, Mom later procured a second cow. Besides being responsible for two cows, I became surrogate mother to seventeen cats who followed me single file to the barn each and every time I went to milk the cows. They all expected me to squirt fresh warm milk directly into their mouths. This was a skill I developed after a few years. All of this forced me to learn responsibility very quickly, which no kid should have to endure. In the meantime all my city friends were enjoying loafing around with no responsibilities whatsoever. In future years this became ingrained, causing me to work diligently for long hours, sometimes even on weekends, losing even greater amounts of loafing time. As a result, the people who employed me came to expect results, which I had to produce or they wouldn't pay me. This wasn't enough. I was enrolled to continue the piano lessons I started when I was six, and on Saturdays no less, and I had to

practice about an hour a day during the week before doing homework and before milking the cows. This had the result of causing me to spend substantial sums of money in my later years for opera tickets and other classical music events when I could have been listening to rap music instead. I remember kids coming to my house after school and asking if I could come out and play. My mother told them no, Douglas has to practice the piano, then do homework and then clean out the barn and then milk the cows. By the time all this was done, on top of getting up before the chickens, I was so beat I had to go to bed. Speaking about bed time, my brother and I had to sleep outside in a cabin. Before we could go to sleep we had to chop firewood for the pot-bellied stove in order to keep from freezing to death at night and again in the morning. We were also running short of accommodations for the chickens in the chicken coop and Mom somehow coerced an outcast chicken, who happened to be brown, and who we called Brownie, to lay her eggs on my bed. I had to be real careful when I woke up in the morning. During these years I developed hay fever. We grew hay for the cows to eat during the winter months and when the hay was ready to reap, we went to the fields with scythes, the same as in the famous Norman Rockwell picture, and cut the fields by hand, in violation of OSHA and child labor standards and without the benefit of legal counsel. Then we had to carry the stuff into the barn and load it into a huge pile with pitchforks, causing me great bouts of sneezing and wheezing. My mother then ordered vitamins from Carlton Fredrick's which seemed to help and this also resulted in me spending large amounts of money on vitamins for the rest of my life which kept me pretty healthy but denied me my right to get sick and access social health programs. All in all, the years of growing up on the farm had an effect on me which has lasted until this day. They were good years and the memories will always be with me. If mom hadn't taken us out of the city, who knows where we all would have wound up. It's too bad all kids couldn't have the benefit of having a mother like our mom, God's Gift to our family.
Doug Laaksonen

The Exciting "Go-Vinnie" aka "My Cousin Vinnie"

"Go-Vinnie"
Why do we say, "Go-Vinnie"?
Vinnie becomes our "Cousin Vinnie"
And we say Go Go-Vinnie, cause Vinnie goes like the song
And like the song he never stops until dawn
Cousin Vinnie, everybody's favorite cousin
The man of the hour, the marathon man
Along with the one and only, "blue eyes, yes, yes, yes, man"...
Our number 1 DJ...
Dennis Nardone, host of the "Remember Then-Doo-Wop Radio Show"
If Dennis never stops his music until you drop...
Vinnie never dropping until the music stops
Our Vinnie is a must to see
Meeting Go-Vinnie in action you will never be the same
The music plays on and on and our cousin Vinnie becomes our marathon man
You will try and sit down but Vinnie but he will make you jump up
Dance to Rock and Roll, a mean Hustle, Salsa, Mambo the Lindy Hop
To the tune of "Shake What Your Mama Gave You"
He spins his legs, twist's his body and does a mean sexy disco to "Saturday Night Fever"
John Travolta?
No match for our cousin Vinnie!
In our club, ladies love our cousin Vinnie
Their spouses too
We all love to hug him
He goes on and on
Try to stop him and he'll stick out his tongue
He never tires or complains he is always there for you
He loves his music, to dance, and to make people happy
His favorite song is "I Believe"
If that comes on, you can try to run
Good Luck... Cause you won't get away

A Tribute to My Friends and Family

Jeannie Winner Russo, "The 21st Century Lady "

The fabulous lady, Jeannie Winner Russo. One can't describe how wonderful, generous and caring of a woman that this 21st century lady has been. Jeannie has been a mentor, confidant, sister and my dear friend, throughout the years. She is an awesome, whom has excelled in being a mother, career driven, business entrepreneur. She is an extremely charming lady with a wealth of knowledge and connections to some very prominent people. Jeannie has traveled the world, experiencing and living the life of many cultures and then some. What's so amazing about that is that she tries to bring these experiences back and share them with her clients, friends, family and those who are not as fortunate to see these wonders. It has been said that Jeannie could charm the skin off a snake. I've seen this first hand. Many who meet Jeannie, easy succumb to her charm and sincerity. The stories of her travels with make you feel as if you are "in the movie", far away from any troubles and woes. I guess that's why she's so great at her job. She can arrange and put you in a place that exceeds your heart's desire. Jeannie is of Italian descent, but has an aura this is from a distant land. A place where you are forced to travel to with her when you meet. A trip designed to perfection... to a faraway distant land.

By far, Jeannie has been one of the most generous persons that I have ever met. Her belief is that the more you give, the more you will receive in return. Therefore she does just that! Giving to her, friends, relatives, charities, even strangers. Sometimes her generosity is overwhelming to me! She gives without expectation, which has taught me a valuable lesson in my life. I am grateful for all the lessons, time, and most of all, the ear that you have offered me, your dear friend over the years. Being there through all my woes, ups and downs, and being understanding. When times were low, you made me feel like a queen. Made me also want to marvel at the woman that I am, calling me the matriarch of my time, helping me to feel proud about being a Medici and in awe of my heritage. I do owe you a part of the lady that I have become. I hope I am living proof for you of the manifestation of your belief. That if you give, you will receive even more in return. Well, I know that you are and will be rewarded. God bless you, in all your endeavors, and what you have for me and others in your lifetime.

To My Dearest Friend Laura

It seemed like yesterday we met in our teens
We bonded so quickly, like two peas in a pod
You came from such a faraway place so I thought
At first it seemed as if we were from two different worlds
You from Brooklyn and me from East Harlem, NYC
It's amazing how we never parted
Half a century as gone by and we are still friends
Our love, friendship and loyalty still going strong
We were so different in many ways and yet we mingled
together like bees and honey
I remember how much you loved skating
You were always on wheels twirling, round and round
You were always flying high on a trapeze, never stopping to feel
a breeze
We would laugh together, cry together, dance the night away
through bad and good times
We drank a little too much at times
Me thinking that was fun to feel high
It was I, who thought, I was going off the edge
What sadness my dear friend Laura you were the Unfortunate
one
Thinking you were always my hero
Never knowing you had a demon inside
You did overcome many hardships
You are a symbol to many you have matured
Laura, always so prim and proper
Everything in place, not a stitch out of line
You buttoned down your buttons and zippered them up and
hung them all in a row
The attire never had a chance to say hello
That was the English in you
But it's ok!, cause I loved you anyway
Me not caring, flighty, compulsive, fun loving
You setting me straight like my dear sister but always in a gentle
way
We both had so many trials and tribulations

Time Vanishes Like a Rose

My dear Laura, you were lost for a while...
But with courage, faith, and most of all endurance you found peace and happiness
Through it all you gave your friends your time, energy, love and understanding
You touched so many hearts
Many in need of mending
They will never forget you
Nor I
You are so loved by family, friends, and grandchildren
It's been quite a feat what you have accomplished in your lifetime
I know when you needed a hug and a smile
I do hope I was able to take away some of your pain
One day, I know we both will be in another place and it will be a safe haven
We both chose separate paths, some good, some not
But Destiny and God leads us home
Life has been good to you and me even at times we did not think so
We are still here
My dear friend, mentor, sister,
Thank you for all the times we shared together throughout the year
Time is of the essence and even if life will come to a close
I know we will meet again on a distant shore
I Love You
Thank you again, for always being there for me...
Brooklyn girl

The Fabulous Patrick Perone, "The 21 Century Elvis Presley"

If you listened to Patrick sing … he would mesmerize you! Such a unique tone, with a great smile, needless to say he is very charismatic. He was the embodiment of a modern day Elvis Presley. Not only was Patrick gifted with a beautiful voice, but name as well. He was named after The Patron St. Patrick, whom was captured by pirates in 387 A.D. The pirates brought him to Ireland and held him prisoner for many years before he was released and sent back to France. St. Patrick was revered for driving all snakes, which were known as devils at the time out of Ireland, he was said to have raised 33 persons from the dead and to have been the individual to have made the sign of the cross! He really was a wonder to many people of France! He lived till the age of 106 years old. Patrick you are blessed! Back to Patrick Perone. Every song he sings really touches the heart. Every melody harmonized through his music energizes the soul. He's truly a blast from the past. His costumes were dazzling, persona engaging. His presence and beautiful music, made him seem like a reincarnation of Elvis Presley! Some may or may not agree, but the feeling Patrick gave me was as if Elvis had not left the building, and was still right there next to me. Patrick idolized Elvis. He dedicated his life to imitating his style and soul. He even purchased a dog and named him Elvis. Patrick's wife Phyllis was also a pretty good singer. Once, together they sung this beautiful duet together that was so heartwarming. They were so in love and were a very talented family. The support of his loving wife and parents spurred Patrick to embrace what seemed to be his destiny… his music. From singing to playing the guitar, which was his hidden talent, they always pushed him to always want to be great. Have you heard the one and only Patrick Perone? Do come out and listen to him, if you haven't. I promise you will want to come back again and again and again. Patrick, keep singing to your hearts content. I want to thank you and Phyllis for the many years of friendship, entertainment and wonderful music that you've shared. Inspiring all those graced to have heard your tone and

The Voice of Harrison Dennis Nardone

Wandering about on a Summer's eve ...
That is what lovers of music do
Searching for fun and laughter
On long summer nights, when the moon is high and the breezes blow cool by
Genre is unimportant
Your music can be Jazz, Classical, Opera, Rock and Roll or Doo Wop too
It just soothes the heart and soul
It is said that it is food
Therefore if music be the food of love ...
Then play on

Strolling along on a warm summer night with an August moon above the sky
We entered into a beautiful park filled with love, blankets, chairs, and food to nibble on .
With a sip of wine
Music played from the 50's, 60's era
Playing happy songs from long ago
Songs for lovers ...
An unrequited love, to set your mood
Taking you back in time
Meeting Dennis Nardone, the host of a radio talk show
One must listen to the voice of Harrison
Listening to his soothing, melodious voice
He will ease your senses
Dennis seeps into your soul from his heart
His blue eyes are like the warm Caribbean Sea
Talking, Listening, to his voice ...
You feel connected to his baby blues
Peering through his sincerity, generosity, hint of humorous side
He becomes that little boy lost and found at heart

There are so many sides to "The Voice" of Harrison
At times his heart belongs to New Rochelle

A Tribute to My Friends and Family

And then who knows where?
He is a multi-faceted man
A man of the year,
Citizen of Harrison,
Talk Show Host,
Honoree,
Medal for "Outstanding work for the Italian/American
Community,
President of the Harrison Chamber of Commerce,
Chairman for Westchester Crime Stoppers,
And now the DJ of all times
By day, he polices the bad guys
Is he tough? Do you think?
Or does he sing the Doo Wop melodies to inmates who has the
"blues"

Dennis, the radio personality talk show host
Hosting the: "Remember the Oldies Show"
Engaged in Politics,
Events of the day,
Crime and ...
Music
Would you say? He is the "Energetic Man of the Year?"
It's hard to disagree
But to be around Dennis Nardone ...
It is a comforting, happy, lovable electric feeling
You can count on him for a song
For you, or a loved one
Call on Dennis for your heart's desire and request your favorite
tune
He will never let you down
I am thankful for all that my friend Dennis have given me
A sense of connection to music, care, warmth and a time to
smile
His passion for people, Rock and Roll, and the Beetles too
All these things my friend has made it a great please to know
and love you

East Harlem Montage, Created By Artist Benjamin Schittone/ Called (Yesterday)

Mr. Benjamin Schittone lived at East 113th st of East Harlem. He is the son of immigrants from Sicily, Italy.   He created this beautiful montage you see here in this portrait of our youth. Inside of the montage you will see a collection of all the people who lived in East Harlem during my youth, helping all those within it to remember the past, and always keep the memories of our loved ones forever in our hearts. It's good to know that Mr. Schittone is well and still creating his artwork. He lives in New Jersey and has a wonderful family. He still dreams about the times of our youth in East Harlem. The photos definitely shows how tight knit we all were, how we mingled, laughed and just had so much fun together. I thought it would never end. Each photo has behind it, a story to tell. Some are gone, but not forgotten. The montage helps us to remember each one individually. If you know East Harlem, look at the portrait! You will see the gas tanks on East 111th st at 1st Avenue, the old Con-Edison building, Jefferson Park and the swimming pool. Remember the concerts, puppet shows and musical entertainment at the White House? The place for lovers to meet. How about Mela's candy store on East 116th st? We danced all night long and hung out every day with our friends and love ones on in St. Pleasant Avenue. Well, all that is also expressed in the montage. Our boys in uniform fighting in World War II for our great country and us girls cheering them on! In it I hope you can see someone you knew from that time. If not this was our youth and memories we shared together in a wonderful area known as East Harlem.
I remember Benjamin always utter this quote by Omar Khayyam, "that spring should vanish with the rose, and youth's sweet scented manuscript should close ".

Thanks for all the memories Benjamin,

                                                              Love Theresa

A Tribute to My Friends and Family

114

Puzzle Pieces from "Yesterday"

If you pay close attention, look through the collection of photos that make up the montage, here are some familiar faces you may see:

Vivian

Vivian was beautiful. Men loved her. She was a tall sultry siren with dark eyes, a cliff chin, long silky black hair; a woman whom from head to toe she was always in place. She felt that she resembled Jean Harlow. Vivian was not an open book. She was extremely complex and never gave a clue to what laid in the depths of her soul. I remember her always trying to be so perfect, even as kids. Vivian caught the eye of my friend Ben and became his first love! Maybe it wasn't meant to be, or the fact that they courted at a very young age, but their relationship was always in turmoil. Needless to say they both ventured on to separate paths and married people who were not from our area. I introduced Vivian to her husband a gentleman from England, and after a few years we just lost touch. I always wondered if me and Vivian were "real friends". Our relationship, as I reflect on it now seems so one sided. One day after so many years I searched for her, we did get to talk and it helped me realize that my suspension was right and therefore I let our story go on like the petals of a wilting flower.

Joe Black

Joe Black was the first love of my life. They called him Joe Black because he had pitch black hair, deep dark eyes, and the longest eyelashes I have ever seen on a man. You wanted to climb into his eyes and get lost there. Joe was loved by all the girls in our circle. He was a quiet, somber, gentle, sincere, honest, wonderful man. Joe got drafted into the navy and served his country well. He was mysterious at times and a man deep into his own thoughts, you never knew what he was thinking! Joe resembled Valentino and to me was the renaissance man of the 20th century. We were very much in love. There is no love comparable to your first love. Joe was my love, my passion, the one I trusted, my best friend. He was always there for me, but I foolish we were in our youth, for we separated for reasons that I could never figure out. Guess "our song" was true, "What a Difference a Day Makes", for one day we were lover and the next a memory. Joe did go on to get married and have two kids that were successful in their careers. Unfortunately, he died at an early age from cancer. To this day I still think of him always, he was a prince to me, and in my heart always mine.

Richard Lapore

Richard was the actor of Pleasant Avenue. He was the wanderer of our gang. Richard was good looking, he had blue eyes, blonde curly hair, and a fair complexion. I must say that he was a handsome little devil. He really belonged in the movies, which later on in his career he did end up going to Hollywood and working in the movie industry. I remember all the shows we would put on together. The "gang" gave us a make believe silver cup, for all the performances that we would put on back in the day. Richard and I both were inspiring actors, but I didn't make it to Hollywood. His family was involved in the theatrical business, and I'm so happy that he got to live out his dream. After, he left for California, we really didn't speak too often. What I do know though, is that he was quite good in his field, started to teach acting and script writing in LA. Sadly, like Ben he too died too young. What a shame for everyone loved him.

Helen Garst

Helen is someone that I consider to be my friend for life. She was my dancing partner and we were extremely close when we were young. We danced all through East Harlem with some of the best Broadway dancers of our day. Helen was a feisty, freckled face, blonde hair, blue eyed Irish girl. We met at a

Presbyterian Church hall. The school that we attended had dancing for teenagers; it was a way in which they tried to help keep us of the streets. It was located in the basement. The teacher of the program looked like she came from an old witch movie. She always wore a long black dress and was mean. Everyone in the school was afraid of her! One day Helen picked a fight with me, she was a fighter, I was not. Since that day we became the best of friends. She was like a sister to me. I remember how artistic, smart and creative she was. I loved her dearly. Helen was from east 115st. and Lexington Avenue. I spent many days with her and her family. They were like a family to me. When I was at her place we were eating Irish, when she was mine we were eating Italian cooking. Today we still talk about the times of our youth. I am amazed at how we never fought, was never in competition with each other, how we were true friends, always concerned with one another's well-being. Helen got married to a friend, named Freddy. I loved Freddy like a brother. They had three kids and were married for fifty years, before he died at the age of 90. Gladly, my friend is still around with me. Reminiscing of our favorite songs, "Stomping at the Savoy", "In the Mood", "I've Got a Gal in Kalamazoo", "Don't Sit Under the Apple Tree". We two were an item, me the Italian girl from immigrant parents and Helen the Irish girl, all American beauty.

Red

Today it may sound boring, but in my time we danced for fun. We danced at school, at home, in church, and then there was street dancing. There used to be juke boxes right out front of candy stores, and we would gather and dance with people from different areas, challenging each dancer to see who was the best. If you were a good dancer, you got the chance to dance with all the guys. There were some really good dancers that would come out doing the Lindy Hop with their zoot suits. One really good dancer was a guy called Red. Red was tall, lanky and skinny. He had red hair and was a really nice guy. We called him rubber legs, because he moved like a rubber band. When we would dance together, he used to throw me over his shoulder, under his legs and any which way he wanted. He was awesome. Red married his childhood sweetheart Mela. We lost touch from our childhood and sadly he past at a young age.

Emilio

Emilio was a handsome, charming, well-dressed guy. All the girls loved him; he was such a ladies man. He was the definition of sharp. Emilio never looked like he belonged in the area. His first love was a girl called Margie Heart. They got married as childhood sweethearts.
Chubby Magleo
No! He was not chubby. I honestly don't know where that name came from. Chubby had a great sense of humor and he also was a great dancer too. He used to promote all of our dancing events. We loved him. He started the first men's club on Pleasant Avenue. It was for guys only.

Mela and Mela's Candy Store

Mela's Candy Store was our Hangout. It was located at east 116th st. on Pleasant Avenue. The owner, Mela, was an Italian lady who was very generous to us. She was short, pudgy, had gray her and such a lovable face. We never had to buy any of the snacks that we wanted, she gave it all to us for free: chocolate shakes, coffee cakes, candy, ice cream, anything our hearts pleased. So we would stay there, eat, talk and dance the night away to the juke boxes music. Mela's wasn't just a regular store, she served food and many desserts. People from the area would come to have lunch and dinner in the booths in the backroom day and night. Mela was like a mom to us. I remember how we would stay inside the store so long that she would yell at us, " Get out you beasties", so out we would go into the cold of the night, and then she would come outside and call us to come in to get warm. She had a heart of gold. I never really knew her last name. Everyone just called her Mela. Well, Mela was a great lady.

Dickie and Julie

Dickie and Julie are the only couple who still lives in the "old neighborhood" today. I ran into them one day near Pleasant Avenue. They both looked wonderful. They are married, have a fine family and held on to the memories of East Harlem.

Me

Theresa Medici. I was called "Savoy". Apparently, it seems that I danced like the dancers from West Harlem from "The Club Savoy", located at 125th st. and 7th avenue. It was an African American area, where all the jazz, great musicians, and great fashions came from.

"The Gang"

Big John, Pete the Tramp, Angelo, Joe Black, Georgie Black, Mike, Emilio, Red, Billy, Richie, Dickie, Benny, The Gyp, Lefty, Angelo the Jet, John and Jim Doria, The Twins, Uncle Jamie, Tweezer, Phil, Stevey Hop, and so much more. Please forgive me for not remembering all the names.

"The Girls"

Dottie, Helen, Mela, Millie, Julie, Vivian, Theresa, Josie, Pauline, Margie Heart, Helen the Irish, Elenore. Just a side not: Dottie, Helen, Mela and Margie, tried to drown me in the Jefferson park pool. I never did get over that. Till this day I am traumatized and cannot submerge my head underwater. No Joke.

Inside the montage that Ben Schittone, our artist, put together that hangs in Patsty restaurant located on east 117th st. and

1st avenue. You can see all the girls and guys from my time in Harlem. All the faces that made history on Pleasant Avenue and its surrounding street still remain alive through its existence. Helping us not forget our past, allowing us to piece it together through the time stamps of yesterday, even as our youth came to its close.

Time Vanishes Like a Rose

A Note of Thanks

I just want to take this time out to thank all those that have inspired me throughout my lifetime. I appreciate all that you have done, supporting me through all the ups and downs, inspiring me to always push forward. I want to give a special thanks to:

Dennis Dion Nardone, my dearest friend, a retired Law Officer, Radio Show host for WVOX and Local National Politician.

Maureen Kelly, my mentor and dear friend, who holds a Master of Arts in physical education. You have always been there for me throught my lifetime. We were more like sisters than friends. Thank you!

Professor John Medici, my brother, who holds a Masters of Arts in Theatre Arts, and a Masters Of Arts in English, whom is also an author, actor and teacher. You have always been an inspiration. The publishing of you first book, "Pleasant Avenue", helped motivate me.

Dr. Joseph V. Scelsa, who holds Masters degrees in Social Studies and Counseling, and a Doctor of Education in Sociology. Presently Dr. Scelsa is the Founder of the Italian American Museum, located on Mulberry St. in New York City. You were my mentor, a very dear friend, who told me to always follow my heart. I am forever indebted to you!

Sheldon Norman, who holds a Bachelors of Arts in Computer Science. Thank you dear friend for all you hard work in helping me to produce this book.

My Journey

In the 1960's, I got married, left East Harlem and moved to the Bronx. I got my first job at the age of 16 in a publishing house called, F.W Dodge Corp, located at 41st street and 6th avenue. I worked in a mailroom doing all sorts of task, mailing, addressing envelopes, and managing all the machines in the office. After a few years, I left and went to work at 9th Federal Savings and Loan Association, a bank in Manhattan located on 42nd and Broadway. My job was a Gal Friday; mortgages, telephone operator, printing, bank teller, operation addressograph, graphotype machinery, mailing room operations, you name it I did it. In between my jobs, I decided to go to modeling school and did a little modeling New York at the age of 17. After leaving the bank trade business, my next adventure was to become a medical assistant. I worked for a private doctor in the Bronx. I didn't know anything at the time about medicine or dealing with people's health problems, therefore I attended a medical assistant program to help me understand my job. That was a quite interesting position and it lasted for 12 years. I took care of so many wonderful people who I began to love. I enjoyed my job immensely. During the 70's I got involved with an old passion of mine ... politics! Everything seemed to be a passion of mine; I had many different interests in my lifetime. While working still as a Medical Assistant, I also attended my club meetings and became president of the conservative party. I even ran for the office for Assemblywoman in the Bronx area. That was a challenge but a moment that I loved and am extremely proud of. I was also on the Nation Republican Committee and had a say in the political field, which I still hold to this day. In my lifetime, I was able to travel to so many wonderful places in the world, Greece, Italy, South America, Africa, Spain, and the Canary Islands, but I can truly say that there is no place like home. I played tennis for at least 30 years of my life. I love the game. I was on many teams, we played in clubs, public parks, wherever, we could. From tennis I have made many friends and met some wonderful people. I had to move on from the Medical Assistant role, for the doctor had decided to retire. I must say that Dr. Marra and his wife were like a mother and father to me. They were the most awesome people that I have had the honor to work with and have as a part of my life. So I applied for a position in a hospital called Montefiore Medical Center. Since I had medical experience that was the way to go, I was on my own now. When I got the job, I applied for benefits for myself and starting planning for the future and when I would retire. I was a secretary in field of nuclear medicine. This was another challenging role for me, but again I grew to love the job and people that I worked with. Taking care of people seemed to come easy to me and be something that I enjoyed. I was on that job for 15 years, I learned so much about people, their problems and medicine. This encouraged me to become a part of "The Sister Servants of Mary", a wonderful cause that helped raised funds for dedicated Nuns and Nurses. Their convent is located in the country club section of the Bronx. They certainly blessed me and I loved them for the work that they did. Helping and caring for the sick. Eventually, I left the field of medicine and decided to go back to modeling. I was a model for an agency that used people to host parties, banks, and liquor establishments. So there I was out meeting people again. Now I spend my days, sitting and writing which is also a love of mine, dancing with the seniors, talking to my friends, listening to music, especially the opera, watching movies and doing all that life has to give. Remember, family and friends are the most important parts of one's life! Live every moment like it's your last, while time vanishes. Thank You!

Theresa Medici